The Townsend Journals

Edited by Andrew Forge

THE TOWNSEND JOURNALS

An artist's record of his times 1928–51

Tate Gallery 1976

ACKNOWLEDGEMENTS

Confronted with the awesome scope of William Townsend's journals and the sense, which I share, that some part of them should be made public, even at this early stage, and with inevitable loss, I must express my admiration for Andrew Forge. He carries out his task as literary executor with an appreciation and discernment that seem to me to be in sympathy with the spirit in which my father recorded his life.

While we are in agreement that only full publication can do justice to the journals, we are very grateful to the Trustees of the Tate Gallery and Iain Bain of the Publications Department for making this interim measure possible.

I am much indebted to Ian Tregarthen Jenkin for his measured judgement on editorial matters. Sir William Coldstream also has stood by me throughout and given generously of his time and attention.

From Caroline Odgers of the Tate Gallery I have learned what diligent research involves and can produce. Amongst the many people who have helped us and made this research fascinating by turning up memories and pictures that have veered from the sublime to the ridiculous, I should particularly thank Nicolette and Rupert Shephard who have put their time, and their photograph albums, at our delighted disposal; Margaret Bennett and the staff of the Slade School, Tommy Carr, Michael Franklin, Peter Fryd, Professor Lawrence Gowing, Mrs Noel Hewlett Johnson, The Reverend and Mrs Geoffrey Keable, Mary Lightbrown, Lady Monnington, Rodrigo Moynihan, Victor Pasmore, Sir Roland Penrose, Roland Pym, Claude Rogers, Anne Stokes, Peter Townsend and Lord Wigg.

I know that in many cases their help has been an expression of respect and affection for William Townsend.

Pauline Key, the designer, has dealt with some very disparate material with equanimity and ingenuity. Our thanks go also to David Nye, Michael Duffett, David Lambert, Fiske Moore Studios, the Arts Council, the British Council and of course to the staff of the Tate Gallery.

Charlotte Townsend

Exclusively distributed in France and Italy by Idea Books
46–8 rue de Montreuil, 75011 Paris and Via Cappuccio 21, 20123 Milan

ISBN 0 900874 97 X
Published by order of the Trustees 1976
Copyright © 1976 The Tate Gallery
Designed and published by the Tate Gallery Publications Department, Millbank, London SW1P 4RG
Printed in Great Britain by Balding & Mansell Ltd, Wisbech, Cambs.

Contents

Frontispiece
William Townsend 1972

William Townsend 1909-1973

William Townsend died suddenly in Canada in the summer of 1973. Besides a considerable body of painting, he left behind him a vast quantity of writing, most of which had never been seen by anyone but himself.

An entry in one of his journals from the early fifties records how, while helping his parents move house, he had discovered boxes and boxes of old papers and notebooks from his childhood. Even he is astonished at their quantity and variety: illustrated descriptions of parish churches, notes on the geology of East Kent, notes on place names, on comparative philology, on Russian Grammar, on bird songs, painting-by-painting reviews of the Royal Academy Summer Show. 'What a diligent boy I was!' he exclaims. This diligent and omnivorous interest persisted remarkably, for the journal in which the discovery is recorded was part of a daily record that he kept with few interruptions from his school days until the end of his life. One can only wonder at the self-discipline and the inner pressure which took him to his desk night after night, whatever the exertions of the day, whether in the studio, or teaching or in a full social life. Some years ago he had realised that this journal was beginning to assume an historic character. He deposited the existing volumes in the Library of University College, London with instructions that it was not to be made generally available until twenty years after his death. At the same time he asked the present writer to be responsible for a first reading and to make recommendations to Charlotte Townsend, his daughter and heir, about publication from it. This was made possible by a generous grant from the Leverhulme Foundation.

In total the journal runs to nearly fifty volumes of manuscript, mostly in hard-covered notebooks of 8×5 in. There must be well over two-and-a-half million words. The earliest entries tend to be a combination of boyish accounts of school life and achievement with highly detailed descriptions of things seen. His two passions are nature and architecture and in these he is evidently much encouraged by his father Lewis Townsend, a dentist and a man of letters *manqué*, a poet and the author of a successful biography of Oliver Wendell Holmes. In much of the early writing one has the sense of a task undertaken to gratify certain stringent parental demands.

Father and eldest son, with or without the rest of the family, were inveterate walkers, birdwatchers, antiquarians, botanists, tireless at the highest reaches of sight-seeing. There were long weekend walks through the countryside of East Kent in which not a nest goes unidentified nor a cottage undated. There were also meticulously planned holidays in Nor-

left
Lewis W. Townsend, *c.*1931

right
William Townsend, *c.*1933

mandy, Wales, Ireland, Brighton, Bath, during which, it seems, every quarter of an hour is accounted for. The first volumes are almost entirely given to descriptions of places seen. The discipline of this kind of writing must have helped to shape his formidable visual memory. It is as though he can play the day over to himself like a film. The painter's immediacy of apprehension combines with the antiquarian's sense of a layered past. And at his best his descriptive writing is distinguished not only in its clarity and intelligence but by a certain dry vividness from which marvellous images suddenly flash out, as when he recalls his first impression of Milan Cathedral as 'a hillside of dead pines', or tells himself that provincial England is 'like a sleepy pear'.

He went to the Slade in the autumn of 1926, his time there coinciding with the last years of Professor Tonks' regime. It was here that he made the essential friendships of his life; with Claude Rogers, William Coldstream, Geoffrey Tibble, Edgar Hubert, Elinor Bellingham-Smith, Anthony Devas, Rodrigo Moynihan, Gabriel Lopez and many others. Two experiences occur during this time which were to have a lasting effect on him. One was nearly nine months of travel abroad, first in Egypt where he was the guest of a fellow Slade student called Yousef, and almost immediately afterwards in France, Italy and Tunisia in the company of a retired naval commander who was an amateur painter. His record of these travels stands as a whole and there seemed to be no point in breaking into it in making the present selection. The second crucial experience was the death by suicide of one of his closest friends, the Colombian Gabriel Lopez. Townsend profoundly admired his painting and his poetry, diametrically different from his own. He had been with him a great deal during the last months of his life and his death affected him deeply. The diaries come to an abrupt stop a few days after Lopez's death. When they start again two years later, we find him back in Canterbury, helping his father keep the accounts for his practice.

Through literary friends of his father's, particularly Eleanor Farjeon, Townsend had built up several connections with publishers and he had begun to find work illustrating books and designing jackets. He had hoped

Group at the Slade, Summer 1929. Left to right: Devas, Clough, Kitchener, Boxall, Shephard, Lopez, –, Scroggie, –, Hunt, Townsend, –

Fancy dress dance at the Yorkshire Grey February 1932. Back row: Nancy Sharp, William Coldstream, Rodrigo Moynihan, far right; Claude Rogers. Front: left side; Edgar Hubert, George Charlton, Caitlin Macnamara, right side; Vivien John, Geoffrey Tibble

to be able to survive on this in London but it was never a regular living. His life in Canterbury has the qualities of an exile, broken only by occasional visits to London to chase publishers, see exhibitions and keep up with his friends. These are melancholy years. He sees himself being slowly brought down by provincial life, losing contact with the people that mean most to him, unable to free himself from the demands of his father, on whom he is, in any case, dependent. He develops a passion for the ballet, blowing his savings and paying a balletomane's court to Danilova and Toumanova in their prime. And as the decade advances, he becomes increasingly drawn into left wing politics, the local Labour Party, the League of Nations Union, the W.E.A., Arms For Spain. Both the Abyssinian conflict and the Spanish Civil War are recorded almost daily, as are the Munich Crisis and the events leading to September 1939. He watches his friends somewhat at a distance, recording with intense feeling each visit and each nuance of aesthetic and political opinion. He is a witness from the wings of their first successes: Devas' rise as a fashionable portrait painter, the short-lived and daring experiments in informal abstraction of Tibble and Moynihan, the founding of the Euston Road School by Rogers and Coldstream and their swift *reclâme* along with Pasmore and Graham Bell in the years immediately before the war.

He joins the army in 1941 and is demobilised five years later, having become a staff captain with the Army School of Education. This period is not recorded in the journals. When he picks up civilian life and returns to writing, he is married, Charlotte is born and he is a teacher at Camberwell School of Art, where William Johnstone was reassembling the people who had been connected with the Euston Road School before the war. From this point on his life is centred on art schools, at Camberwell and then at the Slade where he goes with Coldstream in the autumn of 1949. From 1951 onwards he makes regular visits to Canada where he also teaches.

William Townsend, 'Hedley Mountain'
1963 *Hazel Strouts*

Read as a whole the journals yield an extraordinary picture of a life in both its private and its public dimensions. It is not possible yet to do complete justice to this picture in publication, for to do this would mean to observe a balance between the inner and the outer chronicle. Scores of people are mentioned in these pages and although I do not think that he would have minded the publication of his professional acidities, I know that he would not have wanted confidences abused nor feelings needlessly hurt. So any selection now can only give a partial impression of the scope of the journals and of their final importance – that importance stemming, as I have suggested, from their inclusiveness. The document as a whole is many things: a profoundly honest confession; an acute and sophisticated account of a professional career, with all the gossip and inside talk that implies; it is a succession of passionately detailed and feeling accounts of places and above all buildings seen; it is the critique of an intelligent and humane man upon his times. In selecting these extracts, which amount to the merest tip of an iceberg, I have concentrated on three periods which seem to me to be of the greatest historical interest: his student years, the late thirties and the first year of the war, and the years 1946 to 1951. I have not included anything after these for a variety of reasons. Later entries tend increasingly to be about day-to-day matters at the Slade – conversations with students, college politics, the somewhat repetitive appointments of academic life. All this is fascinating to anyone involved in this world but of limited general interest. These are also the years of his Canadian visits.

He was first invited there to teach at the summer session of the Banff School of Fine Art. It was the first time that he had crossed the Atlantic and all his skills as an observer are brought out to the full. He is learning a new landscape with its own fauna and flora, all of which have to be worked up and recorded. He is learning a new culture, new kinds of cities, new styles of reference. And of course, he is meeting scores of new people and looking at a lot of unfamiliar art. As visit follows visit he begins to understand Canadian life in greater depth and finally even to become a part of it. All his life he had been fascinated by the special problems posed by the relationship of English art to the Continent. Now in Canada he was to encounter similar problems in new terms. He became something of a spokesman for Canadian art and culture and as the journals go on from the first visit to the end, a remarkably rounded picture emerges of a crucial period. But the effect stands as a whole. There seemed to be no point in extracting sections whose real interest lies in their contribution to an organic account, separate to a large extent, from his preoccupations at home.

Finally, during the last few years there is a change in the nature of the entries themselves. The style becomes more elliptical, less reflective, and private and public matters are more sharply intercut. When the time is right for more inclusive publication, such changes of style will fall meaningfully into place. I cannot see that they would here.

One strand which is never dropped in the entire text is his commentary upon his own painting. Whatever else he was involved in, however multifarious his interests, the central concern was always his studio. And yet, like so many artists in this country, there is something tentative in his relationship to it. Perhaps in the end, too much time was spent thinking about it at a distance from a productive *milieu*, his time broken by insecurity, war, too much teaching, his hold on it weakened by lack of recognition. He had committed himself early to a quiet position. Any form of extremism was foreign to his judicious observer's temperament, and he was not an innovator. However, the best of his painting reflects those qualities of balance, sensitivity, and acute economical observation which were essential to him, and in some of the Kentish hop garden series and the cityscapes of Edmonton, these qualities are refined to a pitch which approaches perfection.

Pages from Nicolette Devas's
photograph album

The Slade
(June 1928–October 1930)

22 June 1928

Left to right: Geoffrey Tibble, Edgar Hubert and Rodrigo Moynihan, *photograph by N. Devas*

Edgar Hubert and William Townsend, *photograph by N. Devas*

. . . To-day's event, the Slade picnic. We got to the Slade at the usual time, but the buses did not load up at the gate until an hour later, during which time we were diverted by the capers of [Claude] Rogers, [William] Coldstream and two girls who had provided themselves with the most extraordinary costumes for the occasion.

After a rowdy journey through suburbia we reached High Beech in Epping Forest, where we pulled up outside a large inn, for lunch and any other amusements the place might provide, all of which were exhausted by the end of about an hour. Then on to Rye House with its much wider range of entertainments, from a ruined castle to boating and roundabouts.[1] [Edgar] Hubert, [Justin] Pearis and I started off by having an hour in a boat and exploring the curves of the low-banked Lea, after which we gave ourselves up to whatever was going until tea time. Followed a cricket match and a visit to the gatehouse and dungeons of the fifteenth century mansion. What little is left, the gate and a long range of low outbuildings, is of fine rubbed brickwork, with bow windows on corbels, brick vaults and crenellations on top. The interior is lumbered up with extraordinary clutter, including 'a very fine specimen of an Australian wild dog, the dingo', at present rather moth eaten, looking over the edge of the canopy of Queen Elizabeth's rickety four-poster bed, one of the many the poor woman had to sleep in for the benefit of future generations of sightseers. All very happy, we fitted ourselves into our seats again at half-past seven and drove back, we in the front bus standing up to pelt those in the second with any unrequired object that came to hand, until at nine o'clock we were dumped down once more at the college gates.

Hubert, [Geoffrey] Tibble, [Tom] Carr and I had a wash together and then went off to a party in the studio of one of the girls. High above Wigmore Street were gathered a number of present and past Slade students, some standing about, others sitting round the walls. A table, amply supplied with beer and food was set at one wall. A gramophone on one side, on the other a door to a tiny kitchen where were further supplies and the means of preparing cocktails . . .

24 July 1928

Spent the morning painting, but it was very difficult, for the workmen are now pulling my room to bits and one – a Welsh miner fellow – was sitting

[1] Rye House, a pub in Epping Forest.

William Townsend with Yousef in
Egypt, 1929

looking on all the morning.

Yousef came along and we went together to Bertorelli's for lunch. On re-
turning, some time later, after a useless call at Colebrook's studio in Robert
St. to the Slade I found a message from [E. H. Hamilton] Dicker pinned to
my easel saying that he was just off with Coldstream for a few days in Sussex.
I rushed off to Brunswick Square[1] and luckily found him in, sitting and pot-
tering about in the middle of his glorious muddle. He had been summoned
back from Salisbury by a wire from C. saying that he was off to France to-
morrow, had returned at once, and when he had raised certain objections
against so hasty a departure, C. had decided at once that they would go to
Sussex. Their setting off was most amusing. Dicker alone was in when I
arrived, expecting Coldstream at any moment, when he suddenly discovered that he ought to have answered an important letter, 'really very
important, because it is to a very wealthy second cousin of mine'. He started
the letter, and suddenly rushed off to Bond St. to get an address, leaving
me to explain matters to Coldstream. As D. can never hurry, on any
account, C. arrived long before his return, and after we had repaired to his
basement and chatted for some time and he had packed quietly he began to
pace the room up and down partly amused at so good an exhibition of
Dicker's amazing impracticalness, and very vexed at losing the arranged
train. On his return D. completely disarmed him by his profuse apologies
and explanations, telling how important this visit was – that they had to
arrange a night for the ballet – and then spent a long time debating as to
whether he would take an overcoat or no, while Coldstream stood by almost
kicking him to make him hurry up. Finally Coldstream, with knapsack and
paint-box, Dicker with a large brown paper parcel, and I with Dicker's
easel, filed out of the house, both of the others looking like the robust beer-
drinking wayfarers they detest. When we got round the corner Dicker had
to return for his bathing costume, which took him ten minutes, and then we
made for Victoria, arriving after changing four times on the tube, only to
find that there was no train until 9.5. 'Well it would really be wiser if we
did go in the morning, wouldn't it ? and we would save to-night's expenses,
and if we started very early, really very early to-morrow, we might start
sketching almost as soon as if we went now,' argued D. in his slow, whisper,
though he professed himself willing to sleep in any ditch or hedge, or in the
shadow of a tumulus on the downs, if Coldstream, whom he considers
partly as his protégé, though a tyrannical one, preferred. So nothing came
of it, and we went into a restaurant, drank tea and sat two hours, talking
about a great variety of subjects, leading from tumuli, dewponds and pre-
historic art down to the more familiar subject of modern painting. We
walked back to Bloomsbury, talking all the way, the two travellers having
decided to retire to bed early and so rise fresh.

[1] Dicker's studio was at 18 Brunswick Square.

30 July 1928

. . . I spent the evening chatting with Coldstream and Dicker in the former's room. Dicker was measuring and squaring a canvas part of the time, but when he came down again the conversation took a curious turn. We discussed dreams and their causes and told our peculiar dreams. Coldstream, in his restless nights, when he borders on nightmare, hears or feels pulsations growing bigger and bigger like the approaching throbbing of a machine. I see combinations of shapes coming nearer and growing bigger in a series of rapid jerks – a rather curious parallel. Dicker was telling us of dreams in which he is acutely conscious of an atmosphere – apparently usually a strong heavy atmosphere and from this we went on to discussing the atmosphere of places. Dicker suggested that the atmosphere of a spot was a kind of residue of what had happened there in the past. C & I disagreed and contended – a much more prosaic view, I admit, that it was merely a matter of one's mood, and the associative properties of the objects or the place – their connection with one's own experiences, not those of others. Dicker shewed a curious inclination to believe in psychic pheno-mena and in extreme cases of telepathy. Coldstream laughed in his face and denied that he had any evidence, and I myself am extremely sceptical and put down most cases of telepathy, how few in proportion to the number of people living, to coincidence.

It was when the talk centred on spirits and ghosts that Coldstream broke down, and gave up his rational, sceptical attitude and became uncomfort-able. I was surprised to see this, and amused, though I should have been as bad myself when he told me that, at North Huish where he had been put in a reputed haunted room alone, he had spent three sleepless nights, with a light burning all the time and a sheepdog in his room and an eye on the door.

Dicker sat back in his seat and in a calm matter of fact way told the most gruesome stories of haunted houses he knew of and of murders dating back to the seventeenth century. He makes it all so convincing by giving details of the lives and relationships, names and titles of the actors, and speaks of people with their throats cut and babies burning, without a quiver, or even a smile to bring it down to an easy level, while Coldstream lies on the sofa and beseeches him to stop and I begin to wish I had not got to go back alone to my room after midnight. Dicker tells us that, of course, 'though he would be frightened if he saw a ghost, yet he would really be so very interested that he would forget his fear, and question it'. Despite Cold-stream's entreaties he continued his stories and pictured the former inhabitants of the room, Georgian cooks and house maids coming in a ghostly array to Coldstream's bedside, and leaning over him in his sleep. At this point we separated, Coldstream swearing that he would have a bad night, and insisting that Dicker should stay in his room until he had got to bed.

8 August 1928

Returned with Yousef to town by the morning bus. After lunch and a visit to the bank, I went along to the Slade to see that it was all right for the model who is coming to-morrow.

Went in the evening to see Coldstream. Dicker was out of town, so he was quite glad to see me. He has just finished another still life, with a bowl of flowers and another full of pears, and other objects in a warm colour scheme – very good one, but not quite up to his last, flowers, a pigeon and a bottle of milk, which was excellent. In the course of our conversation he told me of his first oil painting, which he did two years and six months ago. He had a box of paints given him and a piece of cloth to paint on, so he went upstairs and, as he said 'in my impulsive way, I did not know what I was going to paint until I had squeezed the colours out on to the palette'. Then he decided it would be 'Adam and Eve' – all things began there, so he thought it suitable. Without mixing his colours he painted Adam brown to show that he was sunburnt and a man, Eve white to show she was a woman, a child who got muddled up with Eve somehow, an emerald green tree with fig leaves on, and a black trunk. Then there was a sky of pure cerulean, and white round clouds, emerald green grass and that was all.

My first effort was little more than a year ago; one evening at Boxall's, when he was painting, I got a piece of prepared cloth and started dabbing in a landscape. After one other small landscape my next effort was last year's summer composition – not quite so sophisticated, I think, as Coldstream's. His early efforts were very much like Braque or some other of the moderns.

4 October 1928

Dad met me in the morning and we went round to rooms in Brunswick Sq, and then to interview Hubert's landlady – there is a good, top room there, next to one Hubert has taken, which has unusual advantages – hot and cold water in the room, choice of furniture, opportunities for painting. But it is 27/6, which is more than I want to pay. I am left to decide which I shall take. If the latter, I shall pay part of the cash I shall earn by helping Bone.[1] We went on to the tailors, and there Dad left me, as he had to rush off in a taxi to Victoria, to be measured up for a suit.

Bone came to the Slade in the afternoon. The work is to start on Monday week, and I have arranged to go Tuesdays, Thursdays and Fridays; [Rupert] Shephard the other days. The job will probably be finished some time in January. I went to bed, trying to sum up the advantages of my possible rooms, and to decide whether the gain by taking the room next to Hubert, was worth the extra 4/0 or not. I went to sleep still undecided knowing that whichever decision I come to, I shall regret it afterwards. Hubert and I went round in the evening to see Tibble and Carr who have

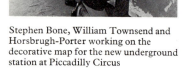

Stephen Bone, William Townsend and Horsbrugh-Porter working on the decorative map for the new underground station at Piccadilly Circus

[1] Townsend helped Stephen Bone on mural decorations in the new underground station at Piccadilly Circus.

installed themselves in a small three-roomed flat in Charlotte Street. Brown was there too, and a friend of Tibble's, and we sat discussing art – mainly keeping down to the old controversy about romanticism and classicism, and to the fundamental qualities of a work of art. Tibble and Hubert think a work of art is great according to its power of evoking a generous human emotion and interest. I argued that this, though enhancing its value is subordinate, or should be to its quality of evoking a purely aesthetic emotion, with no associative or literary interests.

13 October 1928

In the morning down to a show of Chirico's work – his first in England – at Tooths' in Bond St. It is interesting in a way, but gave me no sort of pleasure beyond occasionally a satisfaction in the colour. Its curious symbolism does not seem happy, and the immense seated figures, with short stumps of legs and globular heads, are in a convention that does not bear repetition well.

Hubert and I moved up to our attic rooms in the afternoon, and settled in very comfortably. We are keeping the floors bare, and are having little furniture – Hubert even less than me, for I have a writing desk with drawers that I find very useful for drawings, clothes and books.

Met Coldstream at Carr's in the evening. Hubert went off to the pictures with C. and I walked a long way round with Coldstream to Wigmore St. He has come to the stage of laughing at Clive Bell's theory, as a permanent theory, perhaps not unwisely. I was in danger at one time of accepting it too readily, though now there is a lot in it that I cannot agree with. Chirico is not on the way to a better theory of art – there does not seem to be much good work being done by anybody under 45, and with the exception of Picasso, under 50.

16 December 1928

Slade Dance Christmas 1928. Left to right: William Townsend, Anne Jeffreys, William Coldstream, Hamilton Dicker, Philippa Gee and friend

Late up again – have now recovered from Friday night. Afternoon repainting my prodigal son composition. Went up to Hampstead at 5, but Eleanor was ill. The fare back used up my last pennies, as no money arrived for me this week. When I went to Bertorelli's at eight, as I hoped I found Dicker, Coldstream and [Michael] Reynolds but all were practically bankrupt themselves. I managed, however, to borrow five shillings off Colebrook, and so indulged in a good meal. Joined the party later on at Kleinfeldts for an hour, and then went on to Colebrook's studio, where we had tea and talked from 10.30 until 1.30 mostly about our own psychological problems; our tendencies to sadism; introversion and extraversion; dreams; sensations – and finished up by discussing food and deciding that human flesh might be well worth trying.

17 December 1928

Painted out of my window until tea-time, when I had my first meal – nothing before except a slice of bread and butter, and some tea. Still, it is worth it, to-day being the last free day I shall have in town.

Dicker came along after dinner; and we had the gramophone on, and drank tea.

29 January 1929

Reynolds, 'Portrait of Lord Heathfield', *National Gallery*

After a day's drawing – for Bone had nothing for me to do to-day – Tonks had a look at my drawing and then started off on a fatherly talk which lasted twenty minutes. He started on the lines which every discussion with Tonks takes when he sees my drawing – the contour – then Ingres, who he thinks never regarded drawing purely as an affair of lines, and who had too great a reverence for Raphael – Distortion: as a drawing is a means to an end and not done for its own sake, distortion he considers inexcusable – therefore Alfred Stevens, who made his figures what he imagined the figures of classic times to be was a poor draughtsman. Ingres always drew as nearly as possible what he saw in front of him; all great draughtsmen have tried to do this, and it is only in modern men that we find conscious distortion.

Dutch Show:[1] the Rembrandts disappointing. 'Everyone has felt that. One does not feel in the presence of a great master there. Many of the pictures are probably not by him, they are so dull but the "Jewish Bride" is a fine work.' Then he talked of Rembrandt's development; his early over-modelling, which however he thought a very good fault, as modelling became second nature to him, and enabled him to carry out his better later work in a freer spirit – would like to see a little more over-modelling at the Slade instead of the present undermodelling. Rembrandt would never have been so great had he remained a fashionable portrait painter, and he told me that I should never do anything if I became one, but that I must be prepared to put up with extreme poverty if I did not – no getting into Academies and so on.

He prefers de Hooch to Vermeer, thinks him more of a poet, though without Vermeer's brilliant power over his materials. The Vermeer's at the R.A. as good a representation as we shall ever see.

After this Boxall and I went to the Dutch Show and studied the landscapes there. Met Hubert, went on together to Boxall's room, where after a meal they played vingt et un and I copied a Raphael drawing.

30 January 1929

When I went into Bertorelli's met Tibble at a solitary meal. Joined by Coldstream and Rogers half an hour later, then by Watson; finally Reynolds turned up. Spent two hours discussing our pictures and enjoying a smoke. Went on to Tibble's after he played for us. Then Coldstream came on to my room for a cup of tea, and we chatted until twelve, and decided that

[1] Exhibition of Dutch Art 1450–1900, Royal Academy of Arts 1929.

[20]

conceptual painting was no good. I am still not sure that it is altogether inadmissible – Coldstream is quite certain – but I do not think anyone has ever brought it off successfully.

9 May 1929

Walked down to the [National] Gallery with Shephard, buying a canvas on the way. As soon as we were installed in the large Venetian room, where Shephard and three women had started on copies last week, Boxall arrived and then Tonks. We sat down, and he explained shortly his reasons for setting us on this work, and then chose for Boxall and myself the lower half of the female figure in Tintoretto's 'Origin of the Milky Way'. Before we started he took me aside and hurried me along to the British room to show me 'that at least one good portrait has been painted by an Englishman'. This was the portrait of Lord Heathfield by Reynolds, 'who possessed to a far higher degree than any other English painter the power of the ancient Italians to render the subtleties of form by modelling'. It is mainly on this account, I gather, that Tonks thinks him a more notable artist than Gainsborough. 'No modern painter could do that', he said as we returned through the galleries. 'Why not? Why not?' That is what he wants us to do – make things appear solid in our painting. Not much good in itself, but a useful technical accomplishment.

Tintoretto, 'Origin of the Milky Way', *National Gallery*

T. said good-bye very cheerily and I set to work, and thoroughly enjoyed the study, somewhat to my surprise, and painted on hard until 4 o'clock, by which time I had begun to see a great deal of the subtlety of the painting of the legs, which I had to emulate – the beautiful rhythm of the limbs, unspoilt by obtrusive detail, and yet the amazing completeness of the statement of the modelling of the flesh, and of changes in direction of the surface . . .

27 May 1929

While Carr and I were listening to a little music in my room Coldstream came in. He returned only a few days ago from Greece and to-night was in excellent form. His conversation is clever and usually extremely entertaining and he recounted his impression of Greece and Italy, and the strange man with whom he travelled – admiral, entomologist, autocrat, to all seeming a madman – most amusingly to-night. He told us how, to get away from him and back to England he feigned illness for three days, and lay in bed, feeling perfectly fit without food, until he seized the opportunity when his patron had gone to catch butterflies, when he would leap up, descend to the dining room, have a large meal and return to bed to await his arrival.

30 May 1929

Polling day for the general election. For me a day painting at the National Gallery.

In the evening, [Gabriel] Lopez and I after sitting at Tibble's until ten o'clock or thereabouts went off to Trafalgar Square to hear the first results. There was an enormous crowd, but we could not get near enough to the loudspeaker to hear, or to the screen to see. We next tried the Queen's Hall, taken by the Labour Party for the evening, but could not get in, so made our way to Selfridges. The crowd was solid on the footways and well into the road, so that eventually the traffic had to be stopped to give us space. When we arrived nineteen results had been announced, and gradually one by one more came in, the Conservatives and Labour keeping very near together. Labour gained rapidly and drew ahead to the delight of a socialist crowd which cheered every victory enthusiastically and booed Baldwin regularly. Save for a trip to an overcrowded coffee stall at Marble Arch, where we bought enormous ham sandwiches, we stood in front of the screen until three o'clock by which time Labour had secured a large lead over both the other parties combined so we parted in good mood to walk home – three quarters-of-an-hour of marching for me.[1]

26 June 1930

This morning busy making the final arrangements for to-morrow's picnic, and in the afternoon the annual presentation of prizes. As in every other year we felt sore at the allocation of awards, and outraged at our neglect; but an unreasonable resentment, as we long ago decided that Slade prizes are meaningless honours. Gilbert [Spencer] takes the drawing prize. The last official appearance of Tonks was an impressive and tragically simple piece of staging. At the end of his remarks he stood up and saying 'I do not like saying goodbye, so there will be no official leave taking', walked quietly, with his stooping jerky walk to the door, leaving the long line of the staff, still in their places, whilst we clapped frenziedly, and, for once, with real feeling and appreciation.

Henry Tonks and Augustus John

Strawberry tea on the lawn. Tonks and Steer and Daniels from the National Gallery sit on chairs, at the edge of the crowd, waited on by Bray and Henderson, talking to Guthrie and other visitors, smiling and joking and drinking tea, and eating strawberries and cream. Tonks in his grey suit, looking a grey and tired, but not unhappy old man.

27 June 1930

The Slade picnic. We went as the year before last to Rye House – stopping for lunch in Epping Forest. It was a first rate affair of its kind, and Scroggie and I who had done all the organisation felt very gratified at it. In the evening the usual party – Gabriel, Edgar, Anthony [Devas] and I managed to do our part all right and everyone was in excellent humour with us all again. We took for the night a large room, the ballroom of a small dancing school in Baker St; and so made a triumphal exit from official Slade life.

[1] The Conservatives won the General Election.

[22]

Left to right: Joan Bellingham-Smith, Gabriel Lopez, Roland Pym, Barbara Phillips, Geoffrey Tibble

It went off pretty well – as usual the curious last night of term mixture of old students like Burn, Charlton and his wife [Daphne], unasked arrivals like John Cooper, and a few unknown quantities from the Slade brought into our group purely as a speculation.

When everything was over, Elinor [Bellingham-Smith] stayed to help us clear up. They went to Moynihan's house nearby and brought back brooms, dustbin, water, pails, cloths and we set to work to clear the floors of debris and try to repair some of the havoc done to its polished surface. Having done as much as possible, we stretched ourselves out on cushions on the floor and sofas, and, too lazy to move for a little made Elinor play us Beethoven sonatas on the piano to end everything up on an elevated plane. Trundled back in a taxi at about half past three.

18 July 1930

Venusberg, *photograph by N. Devas*

Rupert Shephard, 'Geoffrey Tibble and William Townsend sketching at Venusberg'

To-day we had lunch in the tangled garden, behind the cottage we propose to occupy.[1] It is overgrown with long grass and nettles, a few seedy cabbages sprout in one patch, near the house are ragged raspberry and gooseberry and currant bushes; a mass of ivy standing monumentally in the centre conceals a wooden lavatory; there are two apple trees covered with green fruit, and elm trees in the hedge. The house is gapped here and there, the upper windows broken, the stairs battered, but it is weathertight and can be locked up, so should be fit to work in. At any rate this afternoon we got Mr Viney to drive his car down with our easels and canvas and settled ourselves in one of the small, windy, whitewashed upstairs rooms.[2]

Anthony stayed at Blashford for dinner. The rest of us went back, and were met afterwards by Joan [Bellingham-Smith] and Elinor. We walked up the lane, across the ford to North Gorley, over the green to the inn and sat outside by a green pond to drink a glass of beer and smoke. On our way back we dropped into a field and under the hedge, around a huge elm bole, settled down; a close agglomeration, until the stars came out and the last men returned past us from the inn. Walked back, a long, arm in arm string back to Ibsley by a straight green streaked lane to the main road, and having left them, wandered back alone. A late peregrination into the graveyard at Ibsley – to vindicate our fearlessness at midnight.

19 July 1930

We spent the morning working at the cottage; which on my suggestion is named Venusberg. My first was Egmont, but Nicolette [Macnamara] considered that too hackneyed, so I changed the key.

In the afternoon Geoffrey and I tried to revive our tennis and played with two visitors who came over to tea – young army men. Fortunately not

---

[1] The cottage was Venusberg, at Mockbeggar, almost next door to the New Inn House where Mrs Macnamara lived.

[2] Mr Viney was the milkman with whom Anthony Devas and William Townsend stayed. They used to paint at Venusberg.

as brilliant as we had feared when we had been told that one was named Hercules and was enormous, and when on their arrival we learned that the other played with a fellow qualified for Wimbledon. Before play started, while G and I were knocking about, early after lunch, on our own, we noticed a foal caught up in the barbed wire of the hedge, cruelly jerked up on its hind leg, torn and bleeding, but perfectly still and patient. We ran for Brigit, Nicolette's younger sister, who spends her life among the animals, lurking in and out of the stables, snatching a meal, tramping out again, with a cigarette in her mouth to her solitary work. Always wandering about, flaxen haired, in her wide riding breeches and a khaki suit, talking little in a low voice, concentrated on her occupation, knowing her way about, not asking for help, but accepting it when it is necessary as a matter of course, (where none would be unbelievable) and therefore nothing to be grateful for. To appearances a masculine young woman, contemptuous of niceties of convention and cultured triviality or even cultured seria; but yet shy and I imagine really very sensitive.

So when she heard she made no exclamation, but came over with us, and together we supported the animal while Tibble cut the wire; washed and disinfected its gashes. I was very surprised by her control, and lack of ejaculation and useless expression of futile sentiments – considering that she is only seventeen.

Gabriel and I went down to the cottage after dinner, and leaning out of the window, looked along the road and whistled tunes from Mozart across the overgrowth of the garden.

Nancy has come down for a few days.

Mockbeggar, 1932. Left side: Mrs Devas, Geoffrey Tibble and William Townsend. Right side: Mr Devas, Anthony Devas, *photograph by N. Devas*

21 July 1930

Morning painting, afternoon tennis with Anthony and before dinner out with Geoffrey to do a water colour.

On our way back we met Gabriel and Anthony who had been giving help after a fearful accident on the bridge just near our cottage. A motorcycle had driven right under a lorry; the man driving it killed, and a girl on the pillion injured. Before I went back to Gorley for our evening meal I went over to the group standing quietly by the ambulance and the lorry. The dead man had been lifted in, and the girl with her broken leg bandaged in pink lint, lay on pillows by the roadside, attended by the ambulance men. With her pale face looking straight upwards, her eyes open and expressionless, black hair combed back around her head, and blue patches clouding her cheeks, she lay so still that she seemed even stiller than the parapet of the bridge; for that is always still, and its quality of repose does not strike us, but a woman is never as still as this even in her sleep. Blotting across the road, and being hastily set with earth, vast flows of blood, creeping from beneath the lorry and the almost unrecognisable wreckage of the still unextricated machine.

22 July 1930

Left to right: Hamilton Dicker, Robert Kitchener, Edgar Hubert, Geoffrey Tibble, Anthony Devas, William Townsend

In the afternoon Geoffrey and I walked into Ringwood[1] with Joan and Elinor; sat by the river, among the willow trees, and met Nicolette and Devas for tea . . . When we got back to Blashford we found [Robert] Kitchener, who had cycled over from Salisbury to see us. I stayed to dinner to keep him company and we discussed at length modern architecture and literature. K. is at the moment a great champion of Virginia Woolf, whose work I scarcely know at all yet; of the Georgian period in architecture and apparently, like Dicker, of tasteful traditional pastiche.

After dinner the other fellows went into Ringwood for a 'blind'; I took Kitchener over and saw them well on the way to inebriation, and then went back, to a long talk on flint implements and cave paintings with Nicolette and Brigit. When Elinor and I left to walk back to Ibsley[2] we found the revellers outside, completely helpless, fighting with their cycles, throwing them one after the other into the ditch, rolling on the grass and shouting with bawdy abandon. Elinor and I had to help Geoffrey back all the way, calling Joan down at Ibsley to give us additional aid, finally landing him safely in his room, where Gabriel had already arrived and was asleep. We had left Anthony and G. to find their way back on their cycles, by the Moyles Court road,[3] and as we walked we could hear their great shouting bursts of laughter, getting more distant as they blundered from one bend to the next through the fields.

24 July 1930

Vivien John on horseback, *photograph by N. Devas*

We all went this afternoon to the Fordingbridge Horse Show – Brigit and Vivien John are keen horsewomen and were taking part, so we had a certain interest in the thing. Huge marquees, light-coloured turf, figures and horses, widely separated, moving in perfect definition in open spaces.

Vivien waiting very erect on her horse near the entrance to the jumping ring, among the cluster of horse-breeders and ex-army riders, her black hair looping down on one side across her forehead, pale and intent; then moving past the rope into the huge circle with everyone watching her as she reined her horse round and moved towards the first jump; her hair flying, her face eager and intent, and starting forward, her body leaning obliquely still and straight against the air. Three times her horse turned from the jump, and as she trotted off, disqualified, among the deprecating remarks of mildly amused onlookers, with her calm, disappointed face surrounded by straight thick black hair blowing out; I thought that some people deserve to win even against better rivals . . .

[1] Ringwood, Hampshire, the nearest town to Blashford where Yvonne Macnamara, mother of Nicolette, Caitlin and Brigit lived at Mockbeggar.

[2] Ibsley, the village between Fordingbridge, where Augustus John's family lived, and Ringwood.

[3] Moyles Court, a manor house in the New Forest.

16 October 1930

Rupert Shephard, 'Slade Life Class'

Old Bedford Music Hall, Camden Town, *Radio Times Hulton Picture Library*

W. R. Sickert, 'The New Bedford', *Tate Gallery*

In the afternoon the Slade summer compositions were criticised. Against all tradition, and Tonks' known views, the Academy was called in, in the person of Sir George Clausen who, in a weak voice that few could hear, toddled round from one picture to the next, solidly criticising each one, to our unutterable boredom. By the time he was finished half the room was empty. I was unwise enough to return after leaving early, and was made to stay to the end; [Peter] Brooker in a desperate effort to prevent a complete fiasco appointing me door-keeper to prevent anyone else from getting out. But [Rodrigo] Moynihan got a second prize, which made all well, for we decided on an evening of celebration. After Bertorelli's, ten of our circle reinforced by [Clive] Branson, who is climbing in among us, and [Colin] Clough, met in the Yorkshire Grey,[1] and in loud-tongued mood moved off to the Old Bedford – one of the last of the old music halls – in Camden Town High St.[2] We took two boxes, facing each other, the really select seats of the place, though working out at only three shillings a head, and revelled throughout the show; Rodrigo, fitly the most obstreperous of all, embarrassed us with loud forced laughs, during the second half, when he came over to my box; while opposite us Anthony rolled on the floor and played with the chairs, and was visited and reproved by the manager in person. So the performance passed, with attempts to flirt with the chorus, while Elinor elicited charming smiles from the handsome young conductor, and Rodrigo embarrassed the wretched comedian . . .

[1] The Yorkshire Grey pub. Parties were held there on the first floor.

[2] The Old Bedford music hall in Camden High Street, now demolished.

[26]

Work in progress on the hoardings for
the Fund for Spain, 1939, *Radio Times
Hulton Picture Library*

William Townsend, 'London Marchers', 1938

'Exile' in Canterbury
(June 1933–August 1939)

5 June 1933

William Townsend, 1931

Father was going over to Bexhill to-day being met at Ashford by Uncle J. who is staying there, and proposed that Geoffrey and I should accompany him as far as Rye and spend a half day there. Geoffrey seemed amazed by the town, not having realised that such places existed, but was not interested in seeing the 'sights'. In a way his is a better method of appreciation at first sight than mine. I go to some place I have not visited before and spend the whole time walking about from street to street and building to building until I have the plan in my head and all the material collected, and usually get stuffed up with plenty of useless material as well as the valuable data; but during the last couple of years I have renounced, or modified considerably this 'collecting' attitude in myself, in favour of the less positive, more fluid attitude of receptivity to emotional material without purposive interests. To-day at Rye we did go inside the church and prowled among the old streets but the interest we found was in scraps picked up by chance in fragments around us. We had lunch in an inn by the Quay – the 'Ship', and sitting there suddenly heard outside old tunes played by fiddle and tambourine coming from the corner outside. G. was very impressed by the performance which sounded sincere and genuine, not a trumped up folk-music, and a new combination of instruments, and we stood in the porch watching the two foxy and rather unplaceable characters who played so well. They had that devilish country slyness and secrecy which might cover even a love of beauty which reminds me of characters in Borrow.

Nearly all the afternoon we drifted about among the buildings and junk of the boat building yards, among piles of timber and boats half buried in the ground, in the furrowed turf that covers the older mud-banks of the river; we found a strange old barge whose deck was like a surrealist picture, with a bird cage, a row of old shoes, a box of pansies growing, and potatoes planted on the deck, around the steering wheel and the ladder to the broken hold. An old women sitting high up in a wheeled chair with her back against the black tarred boards of a shed, leaning on two filthy pillows with her legs stuck out in front of her, showing patches of yellow calves above short black socks, all from where we sat on the ground, piled up monumentally against the sky. We went on discovering in this idle way and talking – about Eliot, then the Pre-Raphaelites, anyone these discoveries suggested – until it was time for tea, and then until it was time to catch the train.

[28]

21 September 1933

Went to the National Gallery in the morning. Igor Anrep was there, with his sister.

In the afternoon it poured with rain and scarcely anybody came to the Gallery, until at tea time Scroggie, MacWilliam and Roland [Pym] came in, with wives and pro-wives, and with the younger Charlton.

Called on Kitchener and Bill before dinner; Geoffrey after. Roland, Barbara and Beck had been feeding there with G. and Teddy. Further discussions on modern scientific ideas, the objectivity of mathematics, becoming, space and time, and the possibility of the artist's intuition being nearer to the absolute object even than the furthest reaches of mathematics. That idea comforts us.

There was an absurd review of my show in the Morning Post to-day, in which ridicule and praise were equally mixed, and both ludicrously expressed.[1] That is Grieg. Disciple of Marriott, otherwise without an idea to rattle in his brain pan.

Tonks came in to the show this morning before I arrived. I recognised him from the secretary's description. Apparently Mrs Wertheim had attempted to tackle him several times to get his opinion of the show and Tonks was characteristically brusque in his replies. There is no one who would less like her ill timed officiousness and transparent concern than him, and I can understand why Mrs Wertheim thought him 'the rudest man she had ever met.'

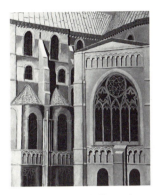

William Townsend, 'Canterbury Cathedral', 1933

22 September 1933

When I got to the Gallery this morning I found a young girl who turned out to be Sir George Gillett's daughter, Miss Dixon's niece. We went out to have coffee together at Ridgways and talked shop. She is a sculptress at the Academy; a pleasant girl but not more than half way to enlightenment in art.

Tried to find Tommy at lunch time as he has just got back from Ireland, but he was out. Walked across the square to Anthony's where I was treated to a studio meal and a little gossip.

A few people came along to the gallery in the afternoon. Stanley Ramsey and his wife whom I had no time to speak to as I was in the toils of two too enthusiastic American ladies whom father had sent along to the show – people who talked and gushed and who never in their lives would buy a picture. Mrs Graham-Baker came in and stayed a long time – a little bewildered I think, but so natural and interested that I found her a pleasant visitor. Not quite deserted by Canterbury.

In the intervals of talking to visitors I chatted with the charming Katerina Blaupotten Cate and found that she was a friend of the Dutch architect Widjeveld and his family, and had spent the last six months in his

[1] Townsend had an exhibition at the Wertheim Gallery, 3/5 Burlington Gardens, London W1, 19 September–9 October 1933.

home while all the preparations for the European Mediterranean Academy were being considered. Widjeveld's hobby is designing, painting and flying kites, which she says are very charming and original – an excellent frivolity for an architect.

[P.G.] Konody put in a good notice for me in the 'Daily Mail'. More generous in length and enthusiastic in tone than I could have expected.

Went up to see Eleanor and Earle. Earle engaged me until E. arrived in appreciative discussions of Tristram Shandy and an analysis of the Roman Catholic faith. I did not stay long, but Eleanor sent me off with a command to buy several copies of the Mail and run back with them to her letter box. She is going to distribute the cuttings to her friends.

Anthony had invited me round after dinner to meet his friend Sue Palmer and her sisters. Roland drove me round with Shephard who had also been invited with ineffectual secrecy. Roland came uninvited, and everyone knew. We spent hours talking, but of nothing very earnestly, and Roland and I outlined the project for a fantastic dramatic production on spectacular and surrealist lines which we fabricated the other day. The Palmer girls are pleasant and quiet, but without much apparent life. They are very rich. Sue is quite the most attractive and has opened out, having sat for a portrait to Anthony, and met us all before, into an innocent and engaging vivacity.

I got to-day a very sad letter from Tonks, a kind of renunciation which I did not want at all. He would give no opinion of my work or any advice, but, telling me I was entitled to my own view as much as himself, and that a view he could not understand, he tells me to leave him to one side and seek the opinion of contemporaries, leaving him now alone to please himself untroubled. This kind of formal leave-taking depressed me more than it should. I knew perfectly what he thought of my work and if he had told me again I should not have been troubled about it, but a declaration of complete estrangement and resignation from my old Professor of whom I have always been very fond, was an unhappy thing for me.

William Townsend, 'Canterbury Marketplace', 1934

20 March 1934

Had intended to go to Gillingham again and start the work in earnest and then carry on to London to see the exhibition at the Zwemmer Gallery which under the title of 'Objective Abstractions' to-day throws the latest work of Geoffrey, Tommy, Rodrigo, Pasmore and a few others to the raging public. It was wet again, so after a morning painting I decided to go straight to town and arrived there and at the gallery, just in time to meet everybody. All my friends seemed to be there except Anthony and Nicolette and Edgar whose younger brother is ill.

There is nothing much to put down about the paintings because they and their painters seek only to please the eye and provide no ingenious solutions to difficult theories other than the simple and natural one of the objective

Rodrigo Moynihan, 'Objective Abstraction', *Tate Gallery*

approach to the picture. An elaborate catalogue with a list of questions answered by each artist proclaims the right of the picture to autonomy, a right the artist must respect – and I agree with this. This seems to me the right attitude to the picture, and not unlike that of Turner at his latest phase or Renoir, except that Renoir loved the things he painted too much for themselves ever quite to overcome them.

After G, T, R, and Pasmore, Ivon Hitchens is the most acceptable of the exhibitors . . . Graham Bell does no more than sentimentalise Geoffrey and show in his answers to the questionnaire an apalling [sic] chaos of thought. Tommy's answers were done for him by Wellington. Geoffrey wrote them first for him, but made them too much like his own to be publishable.

Roland introduced me to a young man named Winkworth (at the Fitzwilliam I think) who is likely to become one of the best patrons of new English painting – he has already bought two of Rodrigo's things and an extraordinary picture by Geoffrey which draws the taxi men to the front-window of the gallery is reserved for him. He has invited me to lunch next time I am in town. I shall make certain of going.

Long talk on communism with Bill, Rodrigo, and Igor Anrep over a drink in Cambridge Circus – Bill gets more and more entangled in the web of circumstances and his conscience – brought us up to dinner time – Bert's.

Roland invited me to join him and Barbara at a show. Went to the 'Country Wife' by Wycherley – not a very inspired production and as a play of that kind, that is to say unrelieved bawdiness needs a good deal of sparkling play to raise it to great levels. It came nowhere near 'Love for Love' which I saw at the Wells last week. If the Restoration dramatists are not brilliantly presented their plays become positively tedious after an act or two, unless one more positively likes filth; if well done they are enchanting. Roland I think was bored and perhaps a little distressed and embarrassed for Barbara (who of course lapped every line of it) as the joke of the whole age was married infidelity and the ingenious creation of cuckolds.

Stayed with Rodrigo and Elinor; as I was back so late and they were preparing for sleep there was not much talk to-night, but I am staying up to-morrow as well.

5 August 1934

While I was at my Sunday morning's gardening Bill and Nancy turned up quite unexpectedly; they are staying at Sarre for the week-end. I was very happy at seeing them again, the first friends I have seen since Geoffrey's wedding, and Bill I have not talked with for a long time for now that he lives at Hampstead it is difficult for me to get at him on my visits to town. They stayed to lunch and afterwards we went out with Father and Peter to Barham, walked through Broane to Denton, had a huge tea which we all enjoyed even more than usual and walked back again as far as Barham. Bill

Broome Park, 1934. Left to right: Peter, Robert, Margaret and Lewis W. Townsend

William Townsend, 'The Pilgrim's Way near Canterbury', c.1934

and I talked all the way of the future prospects and directions of art – for us that is of painting – interrupted by speculation on the chances of war, the nature of new war and ways of avoiding the catastrophe that we see over-hanging London – a constantly recurring theme in Bill's thoughts.

He now seems quite settled in the belief that popular artistic needs will be more and more satisfied by the cinema and that an art of popular appeal, a didactic or elevating influence, calling of course on representation for its appeal, will be in sincerity impossible, – the communist ideal of a mass-appeal art of high quality arising from industrial and economic progress and enthusiasm being beside the point and naive, – so that the real current will be continued only in the efforts of more abstruse painters, working without social references or humanitarian ideals, almost in retreat, aiming at noth-ing more than the recognition of a few people in their lifetime, depending on purchases for galleries for almost all their sales, while the class of illus-trating painters will completely fade out. I find I agree with almost all this, in fact it is difficult not to believe that this is the logical outlook. The realist must see that painting has no new popular future before it of the old kind, now that the film is established, and it is not going to be easy to accuse the exclusive artist working for a small circle and small reward of being anti-social in a new economic system (such as ours under socialism would, un-like the Russian, almost certainly be) where the nation's work would be done by a quarter of the population with the rest free from labour, or by all enjoying most of their time in leisure in a country well directed, and where technical problems are so far advanced towards solution, so that only new organisation is what is required, this is almost bound to be the state of affairs.

Bill is now doing cutting for sound synchronisation with Alberto Cavalcanti, painting in very limited time. I can't quite think what Nancy does. Anthony they tell me goes racing on to success as a society portrait painter.

Tennis at Berry's in the evening.

3 September 1935

Spent the morning sketching at Well.[1] This is a grove of high trees and thick underwoods in the middle of which the Little Stour springs from a pool, fringed with hairlike tufts of red fungus growing from the submerged stems of the trees. Then between trunks of enormous trees and vivid green marshy banks with a straight channel it divides the wood in two. Just out-side the wood are the ruins of a deserted chapel, most of the moulded stones long disappeared, now only a crown of crags of masonry, with elder trees growing within them. Several large trees have fallen down and been left to decay, nettles grow wildly, round another pool, lightning scorched willows lean over twisted with age, leaning to and rising again from the ground

[1] Well, a village near Canterbury.

William Townsend, 'Well', 1935

several times. Beneath one I saw the largest adder I have ever seen. The site lacks no element of the conventional romantic. It has, too, its historical associations and its legends. It is only a couple of hundred yards from the road, but through the young orchards only a dirt path leads to it. I visited it for the first time only a day or two ago, though for years I have seen it often from the road. It is a romantic place that is even more romantic and right in detail at a nearer view.

To-day I received particulars of an anti-fascist exhibition to be held in London this autumn, it is to be not so much propaganda as a gesture of solidarity on the part of serious artists of all schools. [Duncan] Grant, [Eric] Gill, [Paul] Nash and [Henry] Moore are to be among the exhibitors, and I thought I deserved an invitation to show; now I have one. I shall suggest Tommy [Carr] & Geoff [Tibble] as well.

22 November 1935

Henry Lamb, 'Darsie Japp and Family', *City of Manchester Art Galleries*

Left to right: Vivien John, Rupert Shephard, Sue Palmer

To town for the exhibition of water-colours which Nicolette, Vivien [John], Sue and Rupert are jointly holding. Made calls, but ineffectual, on Gibb at Methuens' and on Maclehose; to Geoffrey's for lunch. Geoffrey, after a stern fight had been put up by [Victor] Pasmore and Rodrigo, got his picture hung at the L.G.[1], and has since shared abuse with Rodrigo in almost every review that has appeared. He was delighted with a notice from Frank Rutter in the *Sunday Times* – the first time any one has said what he wanted to hear, and it was indeed a triumph for praise of their honesty followed immediately on a paragraph in which Ben Nicholson was accused of practising deception, cheating by compromise with a third dimension in his reliefs. Rodrigo has sold a drawing and Pasmore a painting to Kenneth Clark...

When we got back to the gallery after tea, Vivien (her gigantic orchid must have been the first seen in the Lyons shop) rang up Augustus [John] and made him invite us to his studio for a drink, so down we went to Chelsea, Roland [Pym] rushing Nicolette and me down in his car so that we had a private view of all that was to be seen. The studio where Augustus works now belongs, I believe, to Euphemia Grove, Henry Lamb's first wife, who embodies the haggard wreckage of female bohemianism, not quite beyond enjoyment, as Augustus that of the other sex. But Augustus is at least a magnificent and picturesque and warm-hearted ruin. He rose to meet us from the floor of the great studio whose white plaster walls, niched here and there to receive Buddhas and goddesses, stretched up into a dim ceiling. Beside him floated up a tall and languorous girl with a billow of golden hair. While we drank we were shown the model of plasticine and matchboxes of the setting for the Barrie play which Bergner is going to act; a rough blocking out of the masses of cliff and tumbled rock – for the scene is a

[1] London Group. The 33rd exhibition was held at the New Burlington Galleries, Burlington Gardens, London W1.

stormy desert where Goliath and David will fight – for which a large cartoon hung on the wall.[1] We saw also a batch of recent drawings, and there are still excellent drawings among them, some of which were designs for Bergner's shepherd's costume – she is to be David. Of one of these Augustus was very proud, for in her hand he had drawn a crook, a single line, a long, bold and almost dead straight line; not, he told me, drawn in a stroke as a gesture, but a firm and deliberate and truly triumphant line, which he had traced slowly and without anywhere a weakening or shaking. His pride in this line struck me as a good thing, like the delight of the Renaissance masters in the complete possession of their medium and its resources. In just the same way they must have revelled in some supremely simple but inescapable exhibition of virtuosity. Other people had turned up by now, Brigit and Vivien, Rupert, Sue, Igor [Anrep] – we were almost a family group – and a charming stranger named Juanita Japp, and it was time to be moving off for dinner, when Augustus invited us all to go and eat snails with him. At the Escargot in Frith St. we settled down to a long table, Euphemia Grove at one end and Brigit at the other, a curious contrast – the first and last stages of sumptuousness. I sat between this Euphemia and the enchanting Juanita with Igor opposite me and Augustus far down the other side between Sue and a strange dusky silent girl, like one of his own mysterious Irish portraits, and she was, I learned, a peasant girl from Connemara.[2] It was an excellent dinner party, food, wine and company were good, particularly my neighbour who was intelligent, lively and more than pretty. She is of that Japp family[3] which Henry Lamb once painted. I once met her father at Ferndown[4] when Lamb came to dinner; in her childhood a playmate of Igor's – Igor was sitting opposite, and as an accompaniment to his interests in psychoanalysis, as patient and future practitioner, claims a remarkable freedom of speech and gesture, a continual compensation for forbidden display of his private parts, in such remarks as 'Yes, I used to dream about you when I was young, when you were five, I wondered what kind of knickers you wore' – followed up with elaborations. In the end I lost my partner to Roland, for when the liqueurs came round Augustus moved down to my end of the table and I was absorbed in his conversation, while Anthony, who has an itch for linking strangers in godless alliances dragged Roland from his shyness and married him to Juanita.

I made a point of asking Augustus what he felt of the artist's relation to

[1] Augustus John was asked in 1935 to design the scenery and costumes for J. M. Barrie's play The Boy David. Ernst Stern eventually took over the design of the costumes. The scenery itself was found to be quite impracticable on the opening night, and Stern was called in again, this time to re-design the set.
[2] A reference to Kitty O'Brien(?) a daughter of 'Cuckoo', a fisherman of Doolin in County Clare, the Macnamara's home often visited by the Johns.

[3] Painting of 'Darsie Japp and Family' by Henry Lamb in Manchester City Art Gallery.
[4] Ferndown, the home of Gerald and Norah Summers, who had been contemporaries of John's at the Slade. Their household made a third with the Macnamaras' at Blashford and the Johns' at Fryern Court. (See Two Flamboyant Fathers, by Nicolette Devas, Collins.)

the public, simply because this is a question which Father and I frequently debate from extreme opposites of view, Father considering the artist as a responsible servant of the public, even if a small one, therefore not justified in being incomprehensible at any time, while I support Cézanne when he says that the only justification for any touch on the canvas is that he thinks thereby to add to the truth or beauty of his work; damn the public. Augustus said, 'What is the public, I never understood what the public was. I always painted to amuse myself and never gave it a thought'. Anthony tells me he is reluctant to give his opinions of living painters and their work, but by offering mine first I found out that he agreed almost entirely, at least over that middle generation between his own and ours, Paul Nash, Ben Nicholson and the geometers. He allowed them talent and even plenty of it, misused, but what he said he could not stand was their pretentiousness, the presumption of their claim to have superseded other traditions and to be intellectual painters – 'I never understood why anyone called them intellectual'. He seconded a favourite argument of mine that such intellectual qualities as they display in their paintings, the purely abstract merits, are all present, exactly the same merits but in a far higher degree, even in such a romantic as Delacroix. Augustus is a very good talker because he is simple and honest, with no flowers of language or high-hat ideas; not the least attempt to exploit his position and pose as an oracle. He is almost pathetically delighted by a word of praise from the young – and that too can be direct and simple!

When the restaurant closed Vivien again appealed to him to keep the party intact and we all went on to the Gargoyle club[1] until that closed too, where we sat and drank and some danced and I between Juanita and Sue, facing Augustus, had all I could ask. One thing only that Augustus said seemed to me to be not perhaps in good faith and that was his denunciation of Sickert – as nowadays a sham. 'He is not in the least interested in his pictures; he sees very clearly what is wanted at the time and does it'. He snorted at his resignation from the Academy and when I remarked that I was glad he (Augustus) had not done the same, so that the show was still worth seeing, he replied 'What do I care whether Spencer's paintings are hung or not? It doesn't matter to me what is hung there. I never sent a thing myself to the bloody place until they elected me'.

So the long evening ended only when again we were turned out at closing time. Roland took Juanita home – (he had his car) – and I took Sue, and went back to sleep at Anthony's where I could get in without disturbance, instead of to Geoff.

[1] The Gargoyle, a night club on Wardour Street remarkable for the owner's collection of paintings by Matisse and others.

20 December 1935

To town in the morning to take some water-colours for Mrs Wertheim who is holding a show of drawings next month. The last one I have done is a good one I think. Saw some drawings of Cocteau's at the Mayor Gallery but was disappointed; mostly scraps and nothing as good as the 'Enfants Terribles' illustrations. At the Zwemmer is an interesting show of recent stuff by the masters of to-day, by far the most exciting being a large and elaborate etching, the first proof, which Picasso has just completed. It is quite unlike anything I have seen of his, made me think of Gromaire, and I suppose it should be described as expressionist; a real victory for Surréalisme and one of the most striking things that movement has produced. Two girls, with a dove in front of them, look down from a window entirely unconcerned and serene, on a woman thrown backwards across what I suppose may be called a horse and who is pointing a rapier at her breast, while over her leans a vast minotaur raising a mighty warring arm. In front stands an innocent looking little child holding a candle, and on the extreme left a bearded nude figure scales a ladder leaning against the wall looking over his shoulder at the curious affair below; in the background is a low sea with a sail and a mottled sky. This kind of subject is familiar enough with other painters. What is not familiar is the curiously detached and straightforward objective way in which it is dealt with, except that the subject is strange there is no attempt at amplification, nothing that is not made clear, even obvious in other respects, great richness of texture for an etching but no stunting technique. It is a work of great force and tragic feeling; real tragedy and not a tragic grimace.

Wellington told me Picasso is himself going through a crisis of spiritual distress. His wife is divorcing him and apparently claiming, as by the law of France, half his property, he is homeless and the representative collection of his work of all periods which he has made to bequeath to his son is likely to be broken up.

Tea with Tommy and Stella. Stella told me very amusingly the story of their marriage, the family interviews, the shocks and their own anxieties. The first time I had heard all the details, now however their parents seem quite pleased with the prospect of grandparenthood. From Geoffrey & Teddy whom I called on next I got an account of Nicolette's & Vivien's show at Fordingbridge last Saturday. They went down for it – Teddy was even called on to take a part in the ballet! – but the performance itself does not seem to have roused Geoffrey very much; he liked the music of Eve Kish and Nicolette's back curtain, otherwise he had little approval to bestow. Augustus gave a good party at Fryern Court afterwards.

Caught the 7.30 to Canterbury. Fog made the train late in arriving at Ashford and there a train had gone off the rails and blocked the Canterbury line. Had to hang about waiting for it to be cleared for hours and finally reached C. at midnight and walked out to Bridge in the fog; a walk livened by a chat with a policeman who flashed a light at me half way. He told me

Baylham, Bathing place, 1935. Anthony Devas, Stella and Tommy Carr

of the prisoners he has to 'deliver' – mostly cases of refusal to pay separation allowances (said he would refuse himself, saw no reason why the man should always pay) – and of how not long ago, having to take a man to Nottingham, found it was the night of the police ball. 'Just as though it was arranged for me. I did not go to bed until three o'clock and I honestly don't know whether I took the prisoner home or he took me.'

The debate on the Abyssinian terms yesterday resulted in their being dropped by the government. Sir S. Hoare has resigned and Baldwin admitted an 'error of judgment' and announced that the peace terms were dead – which Garvin predicted confidently would not happen. There has been an extraordinary outburst of public feeling this week which compelled the government to this course, and although they have saved themselves by making Hoare the scapegoat, there is no doubt that they have lost their reputation, while British prestige seems everywhere abroad to have collapsed badly over the whole affair; even in the city the government is severely blamed and British bonds are dropping. The most unfortunate result however, & an intended one doubtless, is that oil sanctions will be again delayed; this week's discussions having already been abandoned before the date.

23 June 1936

William Townsend and Teddy Tibble

. . . Had lunch with Geoffrey and Serena; their flat now looking very smart, even luxurious, and a garden of shrubs and pot-plants started on the parapets and gulleys of the roof. Geoff was nursing a grievous disappointment which after a little wheedling on my part he confided to me. He had met André Breton at the Surrealist exhibition[1] and through Alma Slocombe, who acted as interpreter, Breton had accepted an invitation to visit Geoff and see his work. They made great preparations, restored frames, borrowed others, prepared food, wines, flowers, cigarettes and waited for him and were brought a message of apology to say that he had had to go off for a lecture at Oxford; he had expected to go by rail, but finding he was being taken by car had had to make an earlier departure. Poor Geoffrey felt that this was the great opportunity of a lifetime slipped from his grasp. He considers himself a real Surrealist, that he alone is working out their spoken gospel in paint, all the other painters barking up the wrong tree. He thinks that Breton himself is a little disappointed with some of the things he has to give his support to at the exhibition – I have no doubt the English exponents do not satisfy – and Geoffrey believed that he could persuade him that at last the great and penetrating surrealist painter had been found. Geoff had prepared a kind of manifesto of his own, a series of pithy sayings and reflections, which Alma had translated into French for him.

[1] The *International Surrealist Exhibition* held at the New Burlington Galleries, 11 June–4 July 1936.

24 July 1936

top
Symphonie Fantastique, Toumanova and Massine. *Victoria and Albert Museum*

centre
Symphonie Fantastique, Massine as the Young Musician being flogged by the Executioners before being put to death. *Victoria and Albert Museum*

below
Le Beau Danube, Danilova

The night at the ballet was a notable one. After Les Cent Baisers we saw the first performance of Massine's new work to Berlioz' Symphonie Fantastique.[1] Even a first performance puts it far above Presages. Massine was the young musician, Toumanova his beloved; and he had provided both with every opportunity for triumph. The first movement I remember least of. The second set in truly opiate ballroom, rich, alluring and a little sinister, with tiers of red arches and candelabra sprouting from the walls, is the most classically formal of all; but good, the dancers entirely in black and white – *tutus* and operatic evening dress. The third movement is a masterpiece, perhaps the best of all, though the fifth too is fine in a different way. The Scene aux Champs has a setting of flat campagna with classical ruins, a great ruined aqueduct stretching far into the distance and a clear washed sky across which Toumanova floats serenely and with great effect in the course of the act, in everything here, the costumes, the dances, the open spacing with comparatively few figures on stage (the other scenes are packed) there is an extraordinary limpidity and graciousness – the charm of our imagined Greece, or better Sicily – to which a single black costume gives an appropriate strangeness. The fourth, the torture scene, has a macabre dance of the judges, slow, the judges first absorbed, triumphant in their pre-concluded judgement, horribly exultant. The tortures themselves do not fail either; but here the action is so complex that it needs to be seen many times. So with the fifth movement with its whirling masses and intercrossing lines of black figures, witches, demons etc. in their swaying conflict with the white robed monks . . .

For Massine it was a night of triumph; for several, but particularly for him. He came to the curtain and made a speech which became something quite impressive through his own and everybody else's excitement. One cannot fail to be moved when someone says 'without exaggeration this is the happiest moment of my life'; when it is Massine the occasion becomes a great one . . .

25 July 1936

. . . I do not know why but we were both in very high spirits; perhaps it was the fact of a children's performance and the release from the constraint of a Covent Garden evening that caused our excitement; or something in the dancers themselves, for they gave an excellent account of each ballet, Danilova especially, dancing with intoxicating abandon and precision in Beau Danube.[2] Every time she points her foot one gets a little stab of delight, the movement is so firm and true and yet full of exuberant vitality; provocative and pure at the same time! And what legs hers are, beautifully shaped, straight at the knee; they are perfect instruments and have the

[1] The ballet was *Symphonie Fantastique* with designs by Christian Bérard.

[2] This was a half-price performance for schools. The programme included: *Swan Lake, Aurora's Marriage* and *Le Beau Danube*.

[38]

hard perfection of fine mechanism as well as the life of superb limbs. Compared with Danilova's, Toumanova's legs are heavy, but Toumanova is superb in her head movements, proud and beautiful; in these she already has a sure mastery: they are swift and decisive and without apparent preparation. Perhaps everyone was enjoying the relaxation from the tension of last night's premiere; whatever the reason they gave a performance for balletomanes with no thought of critics . . .

Gave the Cafe Royal a miss for the first time this week.

9 December 1936

Henry Tonks, 'Portrait of the Artist', *Tate Gallery*

To town. A picture to the Wertheim; a visit to the Cresset Press,[1] who have given me a book-jacket to do for them. Lunch with Geoffrey – late, as Teddy does not rise from bed until midday is well past. He is now painting again, but cannot bear to end his exhibition yet; the date for its close was originally fixed for the end of October, but the pictures still hang on the wall and notices in the corridor still announce the show, with arrows pointing towards the door, to anyone who still shows any interest. He made a success of it in the only way a private show can be a success. He was visited by many interested and influential people, Herbert Read, Clive Bell, Raymond Mortimer, Aldous Huxley, Auden, Grant, Richards, Ben Nicholson, and all these people seem to have been very interested. He tells me that the L. G. exhibition[2] has put a damper on many peoples' interest in modern developments in painting, and that there is a decided swing back from the problems of abstraction, even from the orgies of Surrealism, to the possibility of making a new start from the Post Impressionists. Bill Coldstream & Graham Bell have for instance renounced Picasso and all his works and in despair proclaim there is nothing to do but sit down in front of a landscape and paint it. I think too that that is a much better thing to do than what most of the L. G. members are doing. Bill conceives himself to be the new Degas, Graham is Bonnard over again . . .

10 January 1937

Sir Thomas Monnington, drawing of Tonks on his deathbed, *Slade School of Fine Art, University College, London*

. . . Saw in the paper that dear old Tonks died a day or two ago: though this was my first news of it. It was curious how fond everyone was of him, even those to whom he was most harsh in their youth, whom he misunderstood, and even those who thought nothing of him as a painter. It was so exasperating to be unappreciated by him, as by most people whose opinions one respected, not because one did not care what he thought anyway, but because he told one he could not understand, could not sympathise, and then he urged one to continue along one's own lines without him. That was the

[1] The Cresset Press was founded in 1927 by Dennis Cohen. It produced books on the finest paper with bindings in rich materials. After reprints of the classics the Cresset Press produced editions of contemporary works.

[2] The 34th London Group exhibition was held at the New Burlington Galleries, Burlington Gardens, London W1, 12–28 November 1936.

secret of his success as a teacher of so many good and diverse artists, he did not try to found a school of imitators, – he did that without wishing to out of the weaklings – but when he saw he could help no longer he got out of the way.

24 June 1937

. . . We went on together to the Albert Hall. It was the most impressive meeting I have ever been to, and three and a half hours later when we had to leave to catch the midnight train it was not over and we were sorry to go. Neither Picasso nor Heinrich Mann appeared, but Picasso offered the good reason that he is painting a canvas of the destruction of Guernica for the Spanish pavillion at the Paris exhibition. But the speeches we heard were good, all of them, and the enthusiasm of the audience was terrific. Langevin, for France, put forward carefully all the reasons why fascism must be the enemy of culture and why all the forces of culture must to defend themselves combine now against fascism; Professor Constable summed up the Spanish contribution to European culture and with a passion I had not expected called for its defence; Isobel Brown made the collection and cleverly, as I remember her doing before, played off one group or interest in the audience against another and stirred up rivalry in generosity until every profession, each art, and twenty or more nationalities had sent her donations and messages, even Italians and Germans were among them, with words 'in memory of the Roselli brothers'[1], 'of the international brigade', until our hands were smarting with applauding; but she could not sell the drawing Picasso had given, a recondite little piece of metaphysical abstraction, for which the highest bid was £80. For the programme he had made a fine drawing, agonising; for most people, to buy the other would have been no more than a gesture for the Basques. Paul Robeson was the great man of the evening instead. As there had been some doubt as to whether his broadcast would be sanctioned, as soon as he heard he had flown back from Russia to be here tonight and was properly honoured for it; but apart from such considerations, he dominated the occasion; his personality eclipsed all others as his speech overwhelmed theirs. It was a brave and truly noble speech; the battle front is everywhere, he said, and every artist must take his stand one side or the other, and 'I have taken my stand. I stand unalterably in support of the Spanish government.' That a negro artist could say that in an international gathering and that those words should evoke rapturous applause which went on and on is of impressive significance. Robeson speaks for his whole race as possibly no other international figure does and he bestrode this meeting so that the negroes and the Spaniards seemed the same thing; and then he sang and so easily filled the air and it seemed everything at that moment that he was singing not only for two oppressed peoples but for the oppressed every-

[1] Victims of Mussolini.

[40]

where and all the generous aspirations of the unoppressed as well. It says a lot for Haldane, who spoke after him, that he was able to make a speech which was as courageous and as lofty in its passion and which could still stir a crowd already moved almost intolerably. And this today is the only kind of loftiness that matters. Tonight one felt that even in the awful present, where the forces of the past and of the future overlap and both so much that the present itself seems to have no claim to a place, the dark and negative power had been banished already. I felt happy to have had the chance of being for once where I could feel in the centre of the conflict instead of hovering coldly at the circumference, with so much less hope.

5 July 1937

Canterbury had its dose of fascism today. Mosley at the Forester's Hall. The Keables and all our Peacemaker group except David, with a few reinforcements from Wye College and from Sandwich, went down as an opposition body, determined to remain unprovoked and make no interruptions; in that we succeeded; but three quarters of the audience was opposition which refused to clap for any point of the speech or a penny for the collection, and for the most part remained solidly silent, but some of them could not stand the abuse that was handed out and towards the end of the meeting, after three hours! This led to a few scuffles with the gangster stewards, grimacing at every interrupter as though they were all dictators already, to a couple of ejections and a blow on the head from a baton for one young fellow. Mosley's speech was a very clever one indeed, facts beautifully twisted, but when he had got his agricultural policy put across he was clearly out to provoke bad feeling and make excuses for abuse and shouting and whipping up his own followers to enthusiasm. He never hesitated to call an interrupter a bone-head, village idiot, puppet who was preventing 'this large and intelligent audience' from listening to him. Two-thirds at least must have been bone-heads as they clearly did not like him. The pity was that so much of the heckling was the fruit of exasperation and was therefore disordered and inffective; but one of our Wye friends was persistent and to the point, and being embedded in a mass of supporters was not put out of the hall even after the twentieth remark . . . Trickiness is Mosley's greatest virtue; he is not a magnetic personality – even striding down Canterbury's peaceful high street with his bodyguard.

8 July 1937

With W to the show of ballet designs by Benois at Tooth's – all the Petroushka sets and costumes. The figures are good drawings as well as superb theatre designing; then to the show of new Matisse paintings at Rosenberg's[1] – and someone very like Matisse himself was in the gallery at the time. This is a wonderful show. Matisse in 1937 is painting as surely as

[1]Rosenberg & Helft Ltd which was at 31 Bruton Street, London W1.

H. Matisse, 'Draped Nude',
Tate Gallery © S.P.A.D.E.M. Paris, 1976

ever, which is perhaps not so surprising as the fact that every one of his pictures here is as fresh as though the subject was seen for the first time, and yet they are the same women with patterned dresses and shawls and flowers and stripes. He goes on painting them over and over again and one is never sorry to see more of them. The marvellous patches, the right shape and the right colour first time, all working in together and always a new surprise, and with all the life, not of things deeply felt, but of things seen. The life of Impressionism without its embodiment in matter and atmosphere . . .

We went on to a show at Agnew's of contemporary painting chosen by Duncan Grant and Vanessa Bell; there is a strong family resemblance and you can see that there is a real school of that kind of painting that Grant leads in; but it is not very good. Coldstream, with a couple of austere, capable but rather dull portraits. Rogers and Pasmore are included; and I found their work the most likeable. Tommy was very depressed with the rest of it, and it is depressing to think that perhaps my friends too may with success become as easily satisfied with their work as almost all English painters do. Feel they are almost all amateurs whose aim is status and the pleasures of the artist's life and pleasant things around . . .

18 November 1937

Some publishers in the morning – dud ones I fear; a more dismal weather even than yesterday, at two o'clock it was dark. To an exhibition of Chinese woodcuts and cartoons, organised by the Artists Intern. Association[1] in Constable's house;[2] made very white and bright now. The work is all of the last few years, during which a school of woodcutters in the European manner has grown up; it is left wing and popular; as their own apologist says the movement is in transition now. The more interesting work to me was in the books exhibited, picture books and stories illustrated by series of drawings and cartoons. These, in line, with a brush or bamboo pen, I suppose, are thoroughly Chinese, they seem to be in a style that is just as effective as propaganda as the woodcuts and they certainly have more beauty. The notched, elbowed lines, spiky compositions, the intense vitality; the qualities of Chinese and Japanese sketch books are all found in some of these cheap productions illustrating types of workers, shops, streets; sordid (no doubt satirical) tales of merchants and fun girls, etc . . .

William Townsend, 'On the River Thames'

26 November 1937

Got back to Canterbury in the middle of the morning and spent the rest of the day doing drawings in the streets; stimulated to this by those little Chinese books of drawings of towns and people which I saw in town. A

[1] Founded as Artists International in 1933 in Misha Black's studio at Seven Dials, London WC2.   [2] 76 Charlotte Street, now demolished.

similar pictorial reportage of the appearance and the life of a provincial town would be very interesting, too – or could be, I thought to-day. In the outskirts the Georgian houses with their walled gardens and the gentlemen's retreats wrecked in suburban development, the neglected graveyards in the poor quarters, the children's playing grounds, the cinemas, the traffic, the preachers in the empty churches, the Labour committee rooms and the Conservative Club, the petrol pumps, hoardings, buses, the old houses, the antique dealers and the men playing gramophones in the street. A chaos of activity without direction, rich in errors, absurdity and a forlorn kind of poetry.

I thought of a series of drawings, as objective as possible, simple so that everyone could see what they were about, in pure line; interiors, exteriors, people working and playing, and the ideas would come from them just as they do when you walk through the streets from poor to rich quarters and in and out of shops and houses.

16 March 1938

Left to right: William Townsend, Graham Bell, Gabriel White

Sir William Coldstream, 'Mrs Inez Spender', *Tate Gallery*

The news gets worse and worse. The rebel forces supplied with great new forces of Italian and German troops and aircraft are advancing many miles a day towards Catalonia to cut down to the sea the neck between Valencia and Barcelona . . .

Met Juanita at the London Gallery, which [Roland] Penrose has bought and where she is now working . . . We walked round the lake in St. James's Park, had dinner at Cervantes and went on to a debate, an A.I.A. affair, between the Surrealists and the Realists; Penrose, [Julian] Trevelyan and Humphrey Jennings representing the former and Graham [Bell], Bill and a man named [Peter] Peri . . . Stuck up behind the speakers were examples of the two schools. I confess that the work of my friends, honest to goodness enough and intelligent, looked pretty dull there. The others had the unfair advantage of a Picasso and a Miro! The Surrealists, too, were by far the more brilliant, fluent and well-prepared team of debaters, and Penrose was really quite successful in calling forth the merits of his favoured exhibits. Peri put forward, in very halting English unhappily, an admirable case for Socialist Realism as against Surrealism, but Bill and Graham were not arguing for that at all. The audience was not noticeably one way or the other, though the Realists did not evoke much enthusiasm. Their tolerance of Surrealism was their strong point, I think – allowing it to be a valuable movement, restricted in its pictorial aims, emphasising and properly calling attention, as the Cubists, the Fauves and other groups did, to one element of a picture-poetry and surprise of finding new poetry – but so disregarding other necessary elements as to have no right to claim, as its apostles do for it, to be the one tolerable form of art for today. Peri was to the point in saying that Mondrian made a valuable contribution when he first exhibited a square canvas divided into rectangular shapes but that when he did the same thing twenty years later he was wasting energy, and in drawing a parallel with the Surrealists . . .

18 March 1938

Anthony Devas, 'Lady Daphne Straight'

Group Theatre, *Trial of a Judge*, producer Rupert Doone; designer John Piper. *Photograph by Robert Medley*

Lunch with Bill who showed me the portrait of Spender's wife which he has just finished after forty sittings. He needs all these sittings not to make time for a long series of trials, errors and corrections but because he works with extreme deliberation. Even when finished the paint is very thin – dry little touches, downward stroking – nothing rich about the paint at all.

When I had finished at the NPG I went to see a show at Wildenstein's,[1] three or four paintings each from a number of young painters including Anthony, Bill, Rodrigo, Graham and Pasmore. There is a very good painting of Pasmore's of two men at a cafe table and other figures behind them; well painted and most lovely colour; for Pasmore an ambitious and elaborated work, carried to complete success. Apart from that portraits by Rodrigo of Baba Anrep, by Bill and Anthony were the best things, and some fresh little landscapes by Vivian Pitchforth. Met Graham and Anthony there – both very scared by the prospect of war which they feel is due to fall any minute, and absolutely angry every time they think of Chamberlain and the muck he is getting us into. They talk with despairing anxiety of what can be done, to stop war, scarcely believing that possible, what to do then when it breaks. Graham would like to be able to afford to lay in food supplies now – a barrel of salted herrings, he has been told, is a good thing.

In the evening I managed to get a ticket for Spender's play 'Trial of a Judge' produced by the Group Theatre, performed at the Chapel-made-theatre of the Unity Theatre. This was the first night – a crush of left highbrows. It is the history of a judge persuaded to abandon justice in favour of the fascists, seeing his mistake and recanting, but too late, too late even to save himself. He shares a fate of the communists, and in his last moments their faith too. Spender calls it a statement and it seemed to me to be clear, dramatic and effective and I don't suppose one should expect anything more from it. Actually it was quite terrifying into the bargain.

22 March 1938

After dinner of mussels at the Cervantes with Rob, I went up to Mornington Crescent to join a demonstration marching to the Spanish Embassy with a resolution of support for the Spanish people. It was called by the youth groups of the Liberal, Labour and Communist parties, of the L.N.U.,[2] the Trades Councils and the Universities. Not a huge crowd but several thousands and we went shouting all the way for arms for Spain and

[1] The exhibition at Wildenstein's was *Cross-Section of English Painting* 1938 (*Illustrating some contrasting tendencies*), March–April 1938. It was important in the foundation of the Euston Road School.

[2] League of Nations Union. Voluntary body in support of the League of Nations politically powerful in the early thirties, opposed to rearmament.

Victor Pasmore, 'Parisian Cafe',
City of Manchester Art Galleries

for Chamberlain to go, right down through Piccadilly Circus, along Piccadilly into Belgrave Square; then the resolution handed in, on again through
Eaton and Chester Squares to finish with speeches near Victoria. Old
gentlemen in their clubs and the waiters at the Ritz drew apart curtains to
peer into the street, in Belgravia little groups of people in evening dress
leaving their houses watched us from each corner and clusters of maids
collected at the area gates. Their ignorance must have been surprised to see
that after the massed Spanish flags and the flags of Austria and Czechoslo-
vakia which headed the procession, we were marching behind the Union
Jack, flanked by the Stars-and-Stripes and the Tricolour. Hundreds of
people, too shy to join the procession – as I myself would have been a few
months ago, or on less urgent occasions – walked along beside us on the
pavements the whole way. At the meeting at the end of the march it was
amusing to notice from faces and remarks around that it irked the communists to have to forgo the singing of the Internationale. No doubt they
were justified in feeling it was their show; there would have been nothing at
all if they had not organised it, I suppose. Goodness knows what is happening to the Labour Party.

1 May 1938

Rob got back today but I did not see him until the evening. Went out for an
early lunch and then down to the Embankment to see the marchers collecting. There were a good many when I arrived; groups of men standing
beside their banners leaning up against the railings, and others all the time
coming in from side streets with rolled flags under their arms and red
favours marked 'Unity' or the Spanish colours in their coats – these are the
favourite emblems this year; and drawn up along the street were decorated
vans and lorries of the Co-op Society be-ribboned and plastered with
slogans. Soon after I got there the contingent from the East End began to
march in with a great showing of red flags and Communist party banners.
In this march, whatever Labour leaders may have wanted, all the opposition parties were marching together, Trade Unions, Labour and Communist
parties, a crowd of Christian Socialists with portraits of F. D. Maurice and
others above them, Co-op guilds – in fact the united front with many
memorial banners to comrades lost in Spain. Gradually the other groups
collected around their banners on the Embankment; groups of teachers, of
scientists, of Left Book Club members, Chinamen and Indians, in fact every
possible section of the Left Movement in every possible dissection and
association was there, and we artists numbered about a couple of hundred.
The Surrealists were immediately ahead of us led by Roland Penrose,
Julian Trevelyan and two others who, in morning coats and top-hats with
masks of Chamberlain covering their faces marched along giving the fascist
salute, followed by a loud-speaker van from which issued the tunes of the
Internationale and the United Front tune enormously amplified and on top

Graham Bell. 'The Cafe',
City of Manchester Art Galleries
The painting represents the Cafe Conte
at the corner of Goodge Street and
Charlotte Street (destroyed by a bomb);
the figures are left to right: the Cafe
proprietor's daughter, Geoffrey Tibble
(seen through the counter case), Victor
Pasmore, Claude Rogers, Igor Anrep
and William Coldstream

Trafalgar Square, 1938.
Graham Bell and Adrian Stokes

Surrealist Demonstration, 1 May 1938
Trafalgar Square, 1938. Left to right:
Graham Bell, Adrian Stokes, Victor
Pasmore

of which perched a great gilded bird-cage with a whitened skeleton inside –
a present from the dictators. Very coherent for the Surrealists and they
must have thought so for they followed it up with a strange construction, a
tall tent on a tradesman's tricycle with a wicker cage full of coloured bal-
loons at the top. So we moved off, an immense file, the red and white
banners gleaming far away behind and before us; so long was the procession that looking back from Westminster just as we were turning into
Parliament Square one could see the banners advancing far across the bend
of the river, away by Blackfriar's Bridge, a mile or more behind us. Up
Victoria Street, through Eaton Square where old ladies sitting well back in
their dim drawing rooms watched the ghosts framed in the windows –
pointing out to children the 'wicked reds' no doubt – we marched on into
immense crowds in Hyde Park. The platforms were bristling with speakers
and banners over the crowds, six Labour platforms and, properly separated, the six 'Unity' platforms and between them the platforms of those
organisations which through intransigence, pride, eccentricity or honest
indifference would have none of either – the Socialist Party, smallest of all
with the largest banners, the Social Credit group and the black-draped
stand of the Anarchists with Emma Goldman denouncing the Front
Populaire and every kind of political association. Back to Mecklenburgh
Square afterwards to recover, and to dinner at Bert's. No one there I knew;
Geoffrey out of town. Rob did not come in until much later. The day had
cheered him too.

3 May 1938

Surrealist March, 1 May 1937,
Centre: Roland Penrose and Henry
Moore

Spent the whole day until five o'clock telephoning people, waiting for their
replies, following them up, and being always disappointed. The good men
are all too busy; they have to be busy because they are so few but I cursed
them for filling up May 15th with engagements. I went across the square to
see Tawney. He came out to the door, comfortably dressed in good well
worn clothes, a perfect example of an old batchelor happy in hard work, and
led me to his study. The walls from floor to ceiling hidden by shelves of
books and pamphlets and files, a great table in the centre smothered a foot-
deep in more; the windows looking on to the square and at the opposite end
a long table with a white cloth and the housekeeper bringing in salads and
cheese for his lunch, he reminded me of other old men I had met who had
given their lives to high purposes and who under a load of learning had
remained simple and cordial so that they would still ask questions with
interest and enthusiasm, not like the minor specialists merely proferring
dogma – men like Peyrony and Richie and Wilfrid Blunt, – men who
through generousness of heart had never been arrogant, and who though
driven by their work ceaselessly, sat and talked with a serenity and wisdom
that seemed free from strain. I was happy to meet him though he too could
not grant my request; he could not be sure but would let me know later in

the afternoon so I waited in for his message and from the window where I stood making a drawing of the square, I saw him walking across to bring me his note, and felt a great affection for those of our elders who refuse honours and idleness to be our champions.

In the evening I got back to Canterbury and remembered I had forgotten an engagement to take coffee with Poole and see his house in the precincts. Serious as I had asked to be invited.

11 August 1938

Toumanova and Massine gave a superb performance of Tricorne; one of the best of all things; the vitality, the zest and the assurance of both of them were enchanting. It made me think again about Gaite Parisienne and like it less; it is certainly not a period world far off rebuilt as Tricorne is, nor is there dancing to do like this. I had invited myself to Toumanova's dressing room after the performance; she was in a fine successful mood and deserved to be; standing at the foot of the few stairs leading down to her room, with her dressers behind her and her admirers living in the passage; throwing out thanks to all and flinging her arms round elderly balletomanes who were naturally charmed to be greeted thus; although her face was still made up and beaded with perspiration as I have never seen one, her forehead covered with great round drops all twinkling in the light.

28 September 1938

The car came up from Reading for Teddy and the baby and Geoffrey was busy packing up clothes and other things to take home for her. This hurried evacuation of his wife and child had, I could see, converted Geoffrey's anxiety about them, into a generalised panic which included a strong desire to get himself out as well as soon as possible. Bryce Smith's van called to take our pictures too, but his tremendous attachment to his paintings was swamped today and he gladly left me to look after them. As they went off I saw Adrian Stokes standing on his doorstep opposite and soon a van drew up at his door also to take his pictures to the country, whither he is going with his wife today . . .

In the afternoon I went to the National Gallery with Anne [Popham] who was very quiet, almost numbed she seemed. The central galleries were already closed and while we were there some of the others were being shut up, but there were the Goyas and Grecos to see and the Venetians and the French and the English and we managed to enjoy them, and to be interested in the strange manoevres [sic] by which the glass was removed from the huge Van Dyck equestrian portrait. It was pleasant to see quite a lot of people in the gallery and to be able to believe that art was some use in a crisis: that there were some people who thought pictures were the best thing for to-day, – the blackest day of all so far. It seemed to us then the last afternoon before the war. After we had had tea at Ridgways I walked

Adrian Stokes, 'Olive Trees', *Tate Gallery*

[47]

back to Fitzroy St. Geoffrey had gone home with Teddy, should be back tomorrow to get some more things; so I shall sleep at Rob's and paint at his studio during the day.

On the way up Charlotte St. I bought a paper and read of the extraordinary news of the meeting of the Commons. Chamberlain announced at the end of his speech that he was going to Hitler again, that Mussolini had been invited too . . .

4 October 1938

Back to my picture today. I have got on well with it, but it is just now in a rather ugly stage. Met Rob for lunch and in the afternoon went to the Burlington Galleries to see Picasso's 'Guernica' which Roland Penrose has got over here and which is being exhibited for the Spanish Aid fund. All Picasso's drawings for it are here too, drawings in crayon and pencil and ink, engravings, etchings, oil paintings, an immense amount of preliminary work. I still think as I did in Paris that this is a terrible and horrifying work in the same sense as the destruction of Guernica was both those things. The unfaltering ruthlessness and violence of Picasso's methods today makes it possible for him to achieve a force in conveying such emotions as horror and anguish that no one else could command; but it might be as easily turned to glorification of violence. It is like dictatorial powers, dangerous in any hands but part of the modern spirit.

Picasso, 'Guernica', *Museum of Modern Art, New York*

12 February 1939

. . . An 'Arms for Spain' demonstration in Trafalgar Square, called by the Aid Spain Committee which has suddenly become one of the most active organizations. About 10,000 people there; the International Brigade marched in with their flags from the embankment in a little spatter of rain: their massed flags made lovely colours in the greyness of the square, not too much but a vivid signature for the meeting. On the plinth were [J.B.S.] Haldane, Tom Mann, Copeman and others and I certainly never heard more remarkable or more militant speeches. The police were peculiarly submissive and even allowed themselves to be bullied, but there was something a little sinister in that, for last week a similar demonstration was broken up with a good deal of brutality leading to questions in Parliament, and I have no doubt there was a decision to avoid another stink of the same kind. Haldane was more outspoken than I ever hoped to hear anyone be – we are ruled by traitors, 150 years ago Minorca was allowed to fall into the hands of this country's enemies. The admiral of the fleet, Byng, was recalled, courtmartialled and shot, – last Thursday our government sent a war ship to assist in the handing over of Minorca to our potential enemies and he demanded that Chamberlain be brought before a tribunal and sentenced to whatever punishment our laws provided for treason. 'Yes' said Haldane, pointing down to a little group of police 'I see some sort of a spy

Demonstration in Trafalgar Square, 12 February 1939, *Radio Times Hulton Picture Library*

taking notes!' and added that he hoped his speech would be reported and that he would be brought before the courts as he wanted the widest possible publicity for these views. Then he attacked the National Volunteering scheme as 'cynical impertinence,' inviting men to join the mercantile marine while those already in it were unprotected on their lawful occasions. The same government calls men to its service which is responsible for the murder of 70 British seamen; and so on, until he got to the point of declaring that the laws of such a government could not longer be considered binding on honest men. Copeman's speech was almost as dramatic; he too declared that as the unmistakable opinion of people expressed by all possible legal means had no effect whatever on our rulers it was time to take whatever action was necessary to make it effective even if it meant going beyond the law – and we could easily believe that he was prepared to go that far at any moment. There was an exciting minute or two when he stopped and ordered the police to remove a woman who was interrupting from the crowd. 'Do your duty or I shall detail six members of the International Brigade to carry her out of the crowd'; he went on to say that he had seen her speaking with the police at the other end of the square before the meeting, had seen her edged out by the audience three times when she tried to interrupt and three times brought back by the police from behind the plinth. Copeman stood there pointing at the police and waiting until they had 'done their duty'. Tom Mann was in a similar mood, and everyone seemed to agree. There was then a long march to Eaton Square to present a letter to Halifax. It was a very good march, with unceasing shouting which was limited (to) 'Arms for Spain'; it made a wild reverberation in the streets where there were huge crowds of onlookers. Over our heads fluttered a new series of banners – transcriptions into paint of some of Goya's etchings of the 1812 war: done by Graham, Rodrigo and others, and they looked very well. Daphne Charlton was there, but she would not join the march; she was quite bewildered and could not believe our government was really a base one. She wandered off into Piccadilly to watch the procession pass.

Went to Bertorelli's for supper. Rodrigo and Elinor came in with Fredrick Laws (of the N.S. and the N.C.) and a friend. They had been in the Square too and were going on, if they could find a Group Theatre to sponsor them, to see Auden's new play 'On the Frontier'. They asked me to join them and we found someone to give us the necessary permission to buy tickets for the gallery. I had not seen the other Auden-Isherwood plays on the stage, but this one struck me as very effective – It is anti-war but also a reluctant profession of the futility of pacifism for a generation faced with fascism. The scene where the stage is divided and on each side sits a family from the combatant countries, listening to the broadcast of king and dictator, excusing and justifying the recourse of war, was striking, and certainly strikingly like the circumstances of our September crisis – though it was written before then. The symbolic love meetings of the pacifist victims from the two side were the weakest feature – they lost their point by becoming too personal, individualistic and were sentimental. The revolutionary fraternisation of the fighters was infinitely better managed.

6 May 1939

The Unity [Theatre] pantomime[1] is even better than I expected; it slides from broad farce to pathos without slipping up anywhere, and it doesn't lose its punch anywhere either through being so funny. The wicked uncle is as devastating an interpretation of an individual as one could imagine and all Chamberlain's much publicised phrases 'It is peace in our time' 'It is alright this time' 'from this nettle' etc. come in one after another in highly absurd contexts with most sinister implications. But the hymn of the Cliveden set,[2] sung by four motionless and soignés aristocrats with metallically indifferent expression and an enervated assurance of voice is satire that is merciless and magnificent. I had no idea that such a stage had been reached in the development of theatrical propaganda – popular, truly dramatic, economical and unescapable. We enjoyed it with a tremendous sense of freedom and relief; something here that is alive, real and for us all, and not far from good art already . . .

25 August 1939

. . . Had an early lunch with Rob at Colette's bar in Swallow St – a pleasant American style place; one sits on high stools in rows along the counters beside the outrageously smart girls from superior hat shops and a general Piccadilly business crowd. Gave up work for the rest of the day – my work in London being looking for work. Even the galleries were closed – all the pictures at the National are already being packed up. Wandered along Charing Cross road learned at least about the books that have appeared up to date, and then walked on to see Geoffrey. There was a remover's van outside and half his furniture already in it. He decided last night to leave London for good. Can't stand any more crises; so they were up last night until two o'clock packing and his flat was half empty, and notice given, and they were off to their week-end in Surrey and then to rejoin all their goods at Reading, where they will camp at Geoff's home until they can find a house. This will not all the same break the long connection of my friends with 13 Fitzroy St. From September 1st Rodrigo has taken the top floor studio which used to be Geoffrey's before he moved downstairs.

I hung about and helped Geoffrey arrange for the gas fixtures to be moved and the telephone cut off, things he had hardly thought about, and then

[1] The Unity Theatre pantomime was *Babes in the Wood* with scenery designed by Lawrence Gowing.
[2] The Cliveden Set, the name given to the right-wing politicians and journalists who gathered for week-end parties in the late 1930s at Cliveden, the country house of Lord and Lady Astor in Buckinghamshire. They were alleged to favour the appeasement of Nazi Germany.

moved across the street to see Pasmore. He was happily installed in the studio, formerly Duncan Grant's, and presented a very different picture, as free from agitation as could be. He was peacefully painting a very pretty girl, in a wide flat lacey hat, sitting before an easel. This is a better way to spend one's last day alive than Geoffrey had found. I met his friend once before in Bertorelli's and remember a long argument about colour – chemically, physically and aesthetically analysed in painters' terms. We had just as lively a debate on the international situation, but with less disagreement. We were in the best of spirits; she sitting on a great sofa with her absurd but lovely hat and Victor and I lolling in chairs comfortably about tables spread with paints and brushes, in this great room with its splendid height and widely scattered furniture and litter of canvases and easels, and the sunlight beaming in. We were in the best mood in the world. Victor went out to get tea and twopennyworth of butter and we washed cups in the bath during his absence and then all sat down to tea with a workman who was painting the bedroom . . .

Victor Pasmore, 'Girl at a Curtain',
National Museum of Wales

William Townsend at work on a war-
time portrait of Eric Fenby, the
musicologist

The First Year of War
(September 1939–October 1940)

3 September 1939

William Townsend, 'Hopfields', 1939

Mary Baxter, 1939

William Townsend. 'Mary Baxter', 1940

I was doing the practice accounts for Father this morning, when from the wireless set of a car across the road I heard the Prime Minister's statement that we were at war with Germany. A few minutes afterwards we heard the long rising and falling whine of the sirens and our first air raid warning. One or two people started running down the street, a policeman with his blue steel helmet on his back, and a warden with his first aid case. From the Catholic church opposite a young man ran out and shouted to us to take cover as we stood at the door. We opened up the cellar – it has a trap door and means pulling out carpets and things in the surgery, – but it seemed a pitiful protection when we stepped into it; so out we came to stand at the door and watch again; the congregation had not left the church but a few people had gathered at the door to wait for friends inside. A few minutes later we heard 'all clear', and assumed a false alarm. Now what we have been seeing approaching for years, becoming less and less avoidable as one opportunity of policy after another has been lost, is finally on us. The only surprising thing is why it is to-day and not yesterday that we are at war; for it is over two days since the Poles were invaded and invoked our guarantee. Yesterday the House of Commons was very disturbed, and angry about it. It was Greenwood who got the acclaim who called for us to make our promises effective without any more delays.

I missed lunch to join Peter and the others[1] for a last free excursion to the downs. He picked me up in his little car; we collected Connie and Joan Southwood and he drove us to Chilham. There we met Jack and Mary who had been walking all the morning – had scrambled about in a beet field looking for a sheltering ditch when the alarm sounded. Then Peter took us on to Wye downs in two shifts; we walked to the edge and lay there in the sunshine, with a breeze blowing in from Romney Marsh and the sea, and clouds going along wide spaced, high overhead. We were serious but not too miserable for we had all thought hundreds of times of the things that are happening now and argued them over endlessly. We talked of what we were doing and thinking to do, and of how we could keep going somehow through a war some of the things that make life good and not just something to be used for necessary and abominable purposes – to stand against the distortion of values through hatred and fear and make it possible for a few people at least sometimes to do something normal, to hear a few gramophone

[1] Peter Fryd, Connie Groves, Jack Vane, Mary Baxter, co-workers for the W.E.A. Townsend married Mary Baxter in 1941.

records and discuss happy things; a little of what culture and education have meant to us.

We went into Wye for tea; ate plenty of scones and jam and cream; listened to the Unfinished Symphony being broadcast, and then to the King's speech. Very slow and of course only just what would be expected, the words of sorrow and of exhortation, yet after all it was not an easy moment to take equably. I saw Mary fighting quite hard and even tough Connie taking care not to catch other eyes . . .

8 September 1939

Air-raid precautions unit, 1939, *Radio Times Hulton Picture Library*

Lawrence Gowing, 'Portrait of Alfie Bass'

Up to London in the morning to find out what I could about friends and prospects . . .

London looks neither depressed nor enthusiastic; no evidence of strong feeling, not even anxiety, in the people who move about. The streets and shops certainly look strangely different; the large buildings with their lower windows boarded up and buttresses of sandbags against their walls; the plinths of sandbags along the pavements from which the shop fronts rise latticed with strips of brown paper; the notices on the walls, proclamations and directions to shelters; but only official bills of this kind and pointing arrows, no posters of exhortation, no propaganda; special constables and A.R.P. wardens parading the streets and cars with varying labels indicating their use. In general an air of orderly preparation but not of crisis.

I spent the afternoon trying to find friends, but all had fled. Rodrigo had not taken over his studio at No. 13. Colebrook had gone to Eastbourne; Tommy Carr of course I did not expect to find returned from Ireland, but [Lawrence] Gowing's room at the top of the same house was standing open and bright and empty. At the Air Ministry Department I had an interview with one of the camouflage people. He gave me no encouragement that it would be easy to get into that service yet, if ever. In fact, all that is being done is that a register is being compiled of artists who are willing to do camouflage and who could be called on, but being on such a register would not prevent one's enlisting anywhere else and certainly not exempt one from being conscripted. However, I shall put my name down. My best shot was to mention Monnington; if I had known him personally I saw I could have hoped something. It is clear that camouflage has not got far yet, a small band of designing experts is enough, and even the authorities have no idea to what extent they will be required or allowed to extend their activities.

In the evening I had a telegram forwarded from Anthony [Devas] and rang him up. He told me that Kenneth Clark is getting something going in the Ministry of Information for artists – to do propaganda publicity, illustration, etc – and that Bill and Graham are waiting on this and sitting tight on any news at the moment. Anthony has another string to pull and has promised me further information; in fact we arranged to pool. He told me that Roland is the only one of us who has joined up – anti aircraft. Camouflage he says is hopeless. He himself is finding it very difficult to do nothing and impossible to paint . . .

Then I rang up Stephen Bone. He confirmed my general idea of the chances of artists at the moment. He also is in the know about the M. of Information and gave me the address; but that scheme is still only in embryo.

9 September 1939

Most of the morning went in tracking down the Ministry of Information; from one government building I was sent to another, no one was sure where it was, or even knew sometimes that there was such a Ministry. However I did find it, after calling at the Home Office and learning that its location had changed overnight. It is now at the Senate House of the University, but they were no longer giving out posts, nor even considering applications . . .

Down to Canterbury in the afternoon. The train crowded, and the platforms at Tonbridge and other stations packed with hop-pickers starting the season. Two young soldiers opposite me; they were perfectly happy but had no idea of what was happening to them; for the last few days they had been moved about from place to place doing nothing, now on their way to Shorncliffe to guard the hospital; possibly going to Egypt. There was a pleasant friendly feeling among the people in the compartment; we chatted away without any violence of feeling or opinion. Concern for the Poles and hope that something will be done quickly to relieve the pressure on them is the general sentiment at the moment. People are troubled or bewildered by the slow start on the Western Front . . . even here papers that had no sympathy for Madrid's defenders are recalling the glorious memory of that city and splashing its slogan 'they shall not pass'. The slogans of the Spanish war are no doubt appropriate enough in Poland but it is curious to find them now so approved by the enemies of the Republic, just as it is curious to think of Ward Price leading the *Daily Mail* against German fascism when a few days ago his books were boosted by the B.U.F. in their bookshops, and the *Mail* and *Express* had no use for a peace front against aggression.

Hop-pickers on their way to Kent,
Radio Times Hulton Picture Library

11 September 1939

A telegram from Anthony asking me to meet him for lunch. Up to town by the morning train which was very crowded – the service is very reduced from to-day and the trains stop all over the place and are slower so I did not reach London until after twelve. Walked round Bedford St. and that quarter to see what publishers looked like staying in town and which had shut up. Most of them still there so far, but Gollancz closed down except for enquiries; the communist bookshop next door, displaying the *Daily*

William Townsend, A. R. P. drawings of Canterbury Cathedral

Worker in separate sheets, and various photographs and pronouncements, was the only window lively enough to attract a group of people. *Verve* and the lovely reproductions in Zwemmer's windows still spread out for us behind the gummed lattice... still plenty of people to hang round the second-hand shelves in Charing X road, and books ought to sell better than ever with no competition or distractions. Nothing else worth while is open in London – no theatres, cinemas, exhibitions, galleries, museums, no children and no friends left.

Met Anthony in Charlotte St, and went with him to Bertorelli's. Nicolette of course was there. Igor and his sister and two other girls and Leigh Ashton who is high up in the Ministry of Information and from whom Anthony was hoping much. But his hopes were drowned in a moment, for he told us there are hundreds of applicants at the Ministry; all are being turned away and that the personnel sufficient for present needs was carefully picked months ago. Leigh Ashton said he was certain the war was coming three months ago, never had any doubt afterwards, he is convinced that the ratification of the Russo-German pact – not the signing – precipitated the war, but I was astonished to hear him say that he thought Russia would come in against us in the end, against Poland at least, and take part of the Polish territory. I don't know where any evidence exists for such an expectation . . . But how pleasant it was to be there at lunch with old friends and others, people I liked and women charming to look at, talking calmly. One of the most depressing things to me is the de-centralisation from London, which will no longer be the place where it was always easy to meet many friends and pick up one's interests and news. Now scattered all over England and without the means of travelling easily from one to the other – with no art centre anywhere. Now co-operation is so badly needed to help anything of the arts to survive; in peace time such de-centralisation would be very welcome.

Anthony and Nicolette are very shattered; still suffering from the first horror and hating the world they live in; and people too, particularly those who have been stimulated by the excitement to feel alive almost for the first time.

Anthony is going to register as a C.O. when called up if he is not able to get into a job before then. We both agreed in any case that it was a mistake to think of tying ourselves up in the army before we had to. At the moment all schemes for artists are only sketched out and there seems no place for us in the war system but I don't think this will last for ever. I think we should wait and really try to fit in instead of allowing the difficulties to pull us down and force us where we might not be doing the best job even from the military point of view . . .

I came home by the 5.15 train – there are only two evening trains to Canterbury now; from to-day half the service, and late journeys will be in the dark with only the most miserable mockery of a light from the ceiling of each compartment. No children who survive this war should ever be afraid of the dark again; but that is poor compensation for no bright streets and toy shops, circuses or fireworks or trains blazing by.

12 September 1939

Canterbury Cathedral

Dean of Canterbury, *photograph by Fisk-Moore Studios*

The cathedral nave is full of earth, lorries are rumbling in and shooting cartloads down on the floor and now there is a wilderness four or five feet deep between the pillars from the west door to the choir steps. Services are going to be held in the crypt which is also to serve as an air-raid shelter and the earth is destined to form a blanket in the choir above the crypt vaults. Down below the crypt is being strengthened with props and beams like a mine and between the columns there there are set in position huge earth filled crates forming it into separate compartments darkly and solidly closed in. Back to the catacombs. The old glass has gone and the windows are boarded up, the Black Prince is hidden behind a barricade of sandbags; workmen are everywhere filling bags and carrying them, hammering beams and shifting earth. I heard a good many critics of the Dean for this preparation; from the old verger who thought it was witness to a lack of faith in God who could protect his own house (though he thoroughly approved the removal of the glass, which had happened also in the last war when popular old Dean Wace had ordered it), to the ladies of Canterbury shrieking 'why on earth don't they get rid of the Dean', glad of another opportunity of attacking him. I think he is quite right to do all he can to protect people, once he has decided and others have agreed that the crypt shall be an official shelter; and then God may protect his house of course, but the house belongs too to those without faith as well as those with faith; to those who remember Rheims and the German air force in the Spanish war which did not trouble to spare cathedrals if they were in the way.

Met John Austen at Beazley's. He is quite knocked off his feet, ready he says to sign a separate peace on any terms at any moment. Beazley is braver and I strongly supported the idea of holding a mixed exhibition in his gallery as soon as possible as a gesture of belief in the things we have always held to be important and which are certainly a part of what we are meaning to fight for, and so should go on as long as possible. Not much point in growing as spiritually dark as a fascist country in order to defeat one.

Started making some drawings of the goings-on in the Cathedral. It is going to be a long time before any of us get jobs where we shall be paid to do what we want to do and could do well.

26 October 1939

. . . At five I was in Piccadilly, and from there I walked to Mecklenburgh Square. It is the changes to notice, not the sights anyone would come to London to see, which are the interest to-day; the prostitutes in the turnings off Bond St. standing at the corners so much earlier, the usual pairs, now in

London in war-time: bomb precautions, 1939, *Radio Times Hulton Picture Library*

broad daylight and their colours looking sadly raw; lacking the lights altogether sans volupté; the latticed windows closely crisscrossed with pale brown gummed paper which give the streets a faintly oriental look; I wondered what it was that appealed and stirred my memory until I recalled the mashrabujeh of Cairo and there is that same suggestion of secrecy and furtive excitement in the shop windows here. Broadwick St. has been half rebuilt now; two large blocks in dull compromise modern style have ended the ramshackle air of that quarter; Soho Square, like the others is dug into trenches; in Charlotte St, Schmidts' restaurant and the German butcher shop lower down have notices declaring they are British firms whose proprietors are ex-servicemen, Vaianis is blind-eyed and Poggiolis' have a built out shuttering covering their whole window space; Constable's house stands empty save for the ground floor, Rogers' rooms are quite bare and open for anyone to walk into; in short everyone is retreating from some fear or other. The north side of Russell Square is half demolished now and the adjoining part of Woburn Place, and as the East side of Tavistock Square has recently disappeared nothing is left but a fragment of the Woburn Place I knew ten years ago when I was at the Slade. It is horribly dreary now. To these vast blocks of offices and flats built in the new idiom which has eschewed pretence and decoration but which yet lack the redemption of good proportion and pure line, I almost prefer the pompous academicism of French rebuilding. There is nothing in this construction here, except in the cry, that reminds me of, say, Le Corbusier or the later Mendelsohn . . .

16 January 1940

I left the tube at Tottenham Court Rd. and went down to Veglio's to have some hot soup before going home, and settled down in the far corner at the one unoccupied seat of a table where two men and a woman were already seated. I had with me Wintringham's 'English Captain' to read, but interesting as it was I found the conversation of the others a constant distraction as it was an elaborate and obviously well-informed discussion on modern warfare, bombardment and affairs in Finland compared with lived-through experiences in Spain and elsewhere. It was not long before I recognized that the big young man with tangled hair sitting opposite me was John Langdon Davies, and not much later that I came to the conclusion that the other man, beside me, was the author of the book I was reading. When I had finished my soup and cheese I ventured to remark as I left the table that my neighbours conversation was as interesting as his book; everyone was amused at this recognition and I was asked to sit down again and join the table. It was amazingly interesting – though no-one knew who I was the socialist basis was taken for granted the political problems and intentions presumed understood and the talk was largely on military aspects of the Finnish war, on the moral effects of air raids, the effectiveness of rifles, machine rifles and machine guns, explosives. Langdon Davies is just off to Finland. He remarked that he proposed to return in the spring and get to the near East early in June as he expected that would be the area of the next flare-up. Wintringham agreed that his plan was correct but said he expected trouble in the Black Sea or the Caspian before then. Assaults on the U.S.S.R. through intervention in troubles at various parts of the border were clearly what both expected. They were both inclined to think that there had been practically no serious bombing raids in Finland, arguing that even assaults on military objectives isolated from urban centres would have caused more casualties than the tiny numbers officially announced. There cannot have been any great raids like those on Guernica and Barcelona, or in China. Langdon Davies thinks the whole war in Finland so far has been a matter of small-scale engagements only. Both of them I noticed shewed a snarling contempt for ordinary air-raid shelters, which both, and the lady of the party as well, who had been in Spain during most of the war it seems, bore out with stories of Spanish air raids and the way the Spaniards behaved during them. It was nearly twelve when I got up a second time from the table.

25 February 1940

William Townsend, Portrait of Rosemary ('Drac'), wife of Robert Townsend, 1938

Painted in the morning but the result is that I have decided to scrub the cathedral picture down to the drawing again and start afresh – or from a quarter stage. Bill came in and had some soup and looked at my pictures. Like Graham he thought the portrait of Drac was the best, but he liked the one of Rob too – only thought it might be taken further. We had a long debate on the artist and politics and on the attitude of the Communist Party to both. The communists are of course the only political party that has an attitude to art and artists at all. Bill disclaims for himself that kind of moral sense which would make him feel that he must do something about the injustices of the world, the crises, the war, or willing to make sacrifices for a better world. Would like to see a better world but if that involved the loss of the present just tolerable position and freedom for artists he would rather everything stayed as it is. He thinks that to the artist the world as it is is and should be profoundly interesting and lovable – and with that I wholly agree; but that is the spectator's truth and the lover's, and does not involve love of all details or horror of all changes. He wants a world in which there is a place for conservatives, liberals and rebels; and of course whoever runs the world these forces will always be there and usefully. In a communist world, once established, there would have to be conservatives, millions of them, even if they were dialectical materialists and members of the Communist Party; but that does not mean that in years of crisis when decisive actions are undertaken and the emphasis is bound to be peripheral thinking like this is much more than dreaming in politics.

13 March 1940

William Townsend, 'Kentish Stream', 1940

Saw Victor: half an hour's discussion with him and his flaxen-haired amie. He is against taking any interest in the war, politics, etc . . . Against state patronage, official war artist appointments; and as usual vehemently. We are at the end of a century of amateur painting; a period of great individuals who were amateurs, and professionalism will not be established sufficiently to produce anything good for generations. So he argues we are amateurs in the present society, and must be so; impossible to adapt ourselves to the new professionalism, which in any case is not here, but which will hold the future. The war has made little if any difference to him. Outside events never did trouble him much and he doesn't propose they shall now. All my other friends were much more sensitive to the travails of the world and so the war has affected them. For the better I think; made them all more ardent and happier painters.

17 May 1940

William Coldstream, 'Casualty Reception Station, Capua', *Tate Gallery*

Went up to town with two pictures – A.R.P. in the cathedral and a small one I have painted since of Green Court being trenchified – which Bill has promised to sponsor for the war picture show at the Leicester Gallery. Took them straight along to his studio. He seemed very distracted; Graham was there sitting at a typewriter beating out a letter which he wished to spring on the public with his own and Bill's signature, calling the government without delay to mobilize the entire manpower of the country: pointing out the contrast between that state of war in France and the half-effort in England; shouting to be called up at once, to shoot at parachutes or do anything to stop the German advance. The news of the break through into France has reduced him to a state of neurotic anxiety and desperation from which he feels he – and the country – can only be saved by an immediate and heroic change of attitude. Without this he thinks we shall ourselves be a Nazi state within a couple of months; that we are now besieged and should be behaving as the Madrilenos did; not as we are now – with horrifying and wicked complacency. But though there is everything to justify his feeling there seems to be little profit from this turmoil, and little to be effected by such an appeal if we are indeed within a fortnight of disaster.

Elinor, who was up for the day in London, came just at this moment and we went across to the 'Yorkshire Grey' where a few minutes later Bill and Graham joined us. Graham expostulating frenziedly while Bill tried to steady him down, to associate himself with Graham's attitude but reason him away from indiscreet gestures, to save himself from having to, perhaps, walk straight down the street to volunteer, and to allow himself time to make these calculated approaches, soundings and defences which are his invariable preparation for a decisive action. Graham would not hear of all this; snorted at the idea that one's own moral position should be sound first – in this instance Bill argued one could not appeal for everyone to drop his job and be conscripted where he stood without enrolling oneself in something first – but Graham would have nothing of this. Personal position, sense of rectitude and so on were nothing to him beside the possible effect of saying something that might stem the German advance. Graham just saw the massed forces rolling into France, towards Paris, ready to throw forces into England; everything collapsing before them in a chaos of unpreparedness, panic and moral corruption. He was very difficult indeed to talk to; but it was difficult to see concretely what good effect his excitement could produce. This morning it was merely causing disturbance and spreading anxiety among a few of his friends who wanted to get on with their jobs but were not planning to escape unpleasant duties if they had to . . .

Getting difficult to be a landscape painter. Claude who has got all the permits an artist can (from the authorities), unless he is an official artist, is scarcely allowed to open his sketchbook out of doors. Rodrigo sitting down to draw a farm house, after getting the consent of the farmer, has found the police summoned by the same farmer, rounding him up within ten minutes. The farmer was obnoxious, the police intelligent!

31 May 1940

William Townsend, 'Refugees', 1938

12 June 1940

Here in Kent the sense of impending terror is getting stronger, more people every day are shutting up their houses, leaving with all their chattels, or without them, those who are staying making plans if they can, living with a suitcase packed and addresses to get to. The last three days I have spent most of the time packing up the best of my work, a crate of paintings, a box of diaries and notes, some parcels of water-colours that I shall now manage to be without until the war is over but which I hope to find homes for so that some may survive for me if I am here myself. Until some of them are out of the way I shall be feeling a constant understrain of anxiousness. At the moment all I have done with my life and made with it seems to be gathered in this one room. It is a pity, as well as a mistake, to have all my home, children, capital and prospects crammed into a few square yards, and I don't like it.

Yesterday I had a wonderful day. I got some more poppies from the garden, about the last of the year, started on a new canvas and painted all day. I was full of the happiest confidence in myself which extended far beyond what I was painting to anything I could imagine. I felt capable of any responsibility, any action, full of power; and I really was amazingly happy. Decided there was nothing I more enjoyed doing in the world than painting, not even making love.

13 June 1940

William Townsend, 'St. Augustine's College Gate', 1939

Came back from an early morning session at the [Air Raid Precautions] control room to read the paper alone at my late breakfast. I feel very far from yesterday and sick at heart at the thought of Paris being closed in upon and doomed to such awful suffering even if she is miraculously saved. The capitulation of Paris seems to me something too tragic to believe in; so much more than military reverse, or human terror or lavish destruction is involved in the possible loss of Paris, which is to our civilization what Rome was to the Middle Ages and Catholicism and Mecca to Islam, which is the centre of all that is best that our poor Western Europe has done; not only the great creative city but the most generous of all in welcoming what was fine in every other tradition, ideas and persecuted men; so that Paris stood for the future as well in a special way, symbolising the disappearance of national divisions that must someday come, to make us happy. No city could be more beautiful either, and no people could know better how to live like civilised human beings. Somehow the overwhelming dreariness of the struggle for material wealth and power was compensated there, despite the care for a sou, because the city and its people had not forgotten what life is for. They hadn't been ruined by the wicked puritan separation of body and soul, and the animosity we have fanned up between the two; nor were they dogged by the authoritarianism of catholic philosophy. Paris was the best model I knew for innumerable things and I love it. The thought of the French being driven from the city, of the pall of smoke and dust falling over and dimming the lovely streets, the river, the bridges brings tears to my eyes. There is nothing to be done about it, it is the next two or three days that count. If a miracle like that of Jarama saves the closing of the ring, then of course English efforts may be some good, but we can only look on in a fascinated and agonised silence for the next few hours.

3 July 1940

Met Elinor in Fitzroy St. . . . she was going to meet Rodrigo (up like me for a short visit) at Dante's for lunch and I joined her. Sonia [Browhell] came in radiant and having lost an abhorred job at Golder's Green through her employer leaving for safety. She had several weeks' wages for work lost in her pocket and stood us drinks to celebrate. Then Rodrigo came in with Barbara . . . She was merry enough . . . and so was Rodrigo who had just heard that he had a six-weeks' commission from the Air Ministry to paint two pictures (£50) of aircraft. He was more delighted than ever because this turned the table with wonderful neatness on his enemies. A fortnight or so ago Elinor returned one night to Mansbury to find it broken into and occupied by the local L.D.V. headed by a retired colonel in full uniform, who justified their housebreaking by bringing forward absurd charges of spying, possessing swastika flags and so on, hatched up by the suspicious locals thirsting for the blood of bohemian interlopers. Elinor rang up the police who had not been informed of the invasion. Were furious when they arrived at the house and who drove off the colonel and his men with in-dignity. However in the meantime the L.D.V. had rummaged through the house, had come across the transcription of Goya etchings with anti-fascist and Spanish slogans on them which Rodrigo had done for the Spanish war campaigns and made off with them, and they are now being summoned to apologize and return the pictures. If they will not do this Elinor says they may sue them for housebreaking and stealing pictures! Elinor says she has black looks from the villagers, baulked of their prey, which will not be lightened by the knowledge that the proposed victim has been entrusted by the air ministry with a confidential commission.

21 September 1940

A raid warning was given just as we left Tunbridge Wells, and we had reached Ashford before the all-clear. In the car we could hear nothing of the planes, nor see them but we could calculate very well their course from the direction of the upturned faces of the little groups of men and women standing in the village streets, by the roadside, or in knots about cottage gates. It was odd driving through this countryside which I know so well and having the impression that it had suddenly become more thickly peopled. I have never seen so many folk about on these roads, nobody can have taken shelter; but all had stepped outside to watch the planes. Mothers were holding up their babies even at the garden fences to point out the planes in the sky; we seemed to be the only ones indifferent to what was above. Goudhurst Street was a wonderful sight. The hill was crowded with folk, clusters of hop-pickers and groups of soldiers, and on the terrace out-side the pub at the top the benches were black with rows of drinkers, and the pub at the bottom seemed even fuller, the drinkers jammed in the doorway and overflowing into the paved triangle in front of the house. It was a perfect Rowlandson village for the day: more packed with flirting girls and topers than you could imagine anywhere but in his drawings: and for a mile of two beyond the village in both directions girls, in twos and threes, dressed in their smartest, were making their way in.

11 October 1940

Father had promised to come home this afternoon for me to begin a portrait and I had just finished stretching the canvas and was at lunch when he suddenly appeared to tell us that there had been a bomb in Burgate St. half an hour before. He had been attending a patient and all his windows had blown in; the patient was still waiting there and he rushed across the road to catch the next bus to Canterbury. There was something very touching in the thought of this conscientiousness and energy kept up after a bad shock; I thought so as I watched him – a frail little man – running across the road to the bus. I said to Mother as we sat down again, 'It is hard luck to be worried all the time, with half his practice gone, and then to be nearly

Bombed Canterbury, *photograph by Fisk-Moore Studios*

Uden, 'Canterbury High Street the morning after the Blitz'

bombed out twice in a few weeks' and she burst into tears; and I found it difficult not to do so myself in the curious emotion and relief of survival. One feels saved oneself as well as the possible victim. I went into Canterbury. There was a rope across the street and beyond it a crowd of men in tin helmets busy over a pile of wreckage in the roadway, grey dusty beams and rubble; on one side, the side of father's surgery a huge gap where Williams the furriers proud new shop had stood and Carver and Staniforths' bookshop; both now heaps of spiky rubbish with men clambering over, prising up shards and timber, tossing them into the street with a clatter and a puff of plaster dust. Beyond the scarred side wall of Stephensons, the tailors, and the stripped front and the jagged hole of the shop below; this side the gap a torn upper floor hanging into the street and a comb of rafters from the roof cocked above it, in that pile disappeared the bookshop which I never failed to visit when I was in the town, where I was the first customer, where I had bought my books and browsed over many unread, where only yesterday I went in to mention Edmond's poems, to get 'Horizon'; and in that pile Miss Carver had been killed, Miss Staniforth gravely injured, and there was not even a book to be seen. The furrier and his customers were dead too; a woman who had been stepping from her car on the opposite side of the street was killed too; old Mr Dukes the watchmaker dragged covered with rubbish but only bruised from the ruin of his shop; all people our familiars for years, their business our daily interest and this group of buildings our centre in Canterbury. On the other side of the road was the tea shop where we lunched and took our friends to coffee, the Beazley's Gallery where I held my water colour shows, where three of my drawings for Jane were this day in the window; the second-hand book shop; the pub at the corner of the lane where Beazley slipped in for his drinks, and I sometimes too with Tim Jordan – all now with the fronts blown in and knocked awry, with scars and cuts all over and clumps of tiles jolted loose on the roofs. I was allowed past the rope when I had told my name and business; all Father's windows had been blown in, the glass had scattered everywhere about the rooms, on floors and furniture, followed by dust and plaster chips, so that it looked like a house left by its owners and abandoned for ten years to wind and weather. Father was restless and could think of nothing to do, so I started on to clearing up, sweeping first everything on to the floor, shaking the glass off the carpets and taking them out to the garden at the back to be swept, collecting the loose panes that might still fall from the windows; then men appeared to nail muslin and boards across the windows, we had a cup of tea sent in and looked a little more calmly about. Father had to go to see an old patient, and as we walked up to the garage to get into a taxi I saw Mr Beazley, of the gallery, across the road, being helped along by a young man. His clothes were indescribably creased and covered with white dust and pieces of wood and plaster, his face was flaccid, pale, like suet, and his eyes looked tiny, so pitifully weak and watery. He used to be the very type of prosperous looking, stout, confident and comfortable bourgeois, pleased with his appearance, the world and his place in it. He had just been to take Miss Carver's body to the mortuary. 'I wish it had been me. I wish it had been me', he said in a strange, whimpering little voice as though it was all he had left in the world, a hopeless wish, and he was noticing nothing else. Then he shuffled on, leaning on his companion's arm. Miss C. had been his secretary in Paris, his companion for thirty years; once his mistress I always supposed.

It was a wonderful night; the moon almost full again, quite clear and still; the siren came clearly to us from Canterbury. After supper Father and I walked a little way up Bridge Hill as we usually do; and suddenly heard two clattering reports of bombs between us and Canterbury. Father started to run home and I with him, a thing neither of would have done yesterday – not for so distant a report, hard though it came through the stillness of the night . . .

Bombed Canterbury, *photograph by Fisk-Moore Studios*

William Townsend, 'South Bank', 1948

Teaching at Camberwell
(April 1946–May 1949)

30 April 1946

Camberwell School of Arts and Crafts.
Southwark Collection

Victor Pasmore, 'The Hanging Gardens
of Hammersmith

. . . After dinner dropped in on Victor and Wendy in Hammersmith Terrace. They were just finishing their meal under the vine tree in the glazed verandah which at the back of the house looks over the riverside gardens which Victor has appropriated as his favourite subject matter.

Claude has just failed to be elected an ARA and Victor was delighted to think he had been kept out – not at all through any jealousy but because of his contempt for the idea that the Academy can be reformed from within, that it can do anything but corrupt a good painter . . . and because he thinks it does not even offer a new market that is worth troubling about. Victor is an *enragé* advocate of complete independence for the artist; he thinks he should paint just the pictures he pleases, giving no thought to a patron or possible public . . . There is a great deal to be said for this to-day, as through all the 19th century, because, paradoxically, it is only in such an amateur position that the painter, unless he is a very tough dominating personality, can maintain a professional attitude to his ideas and his craft. In the eighteenth century there was a large enough public, instructed enough to understand the standards of the time and to allow that the artist was the expert in matters of painting. The artist could be honest and be paid for it. To-day that public is very small, but there is a larger public who look at and judge pictures which is as dangerous as the academy public; . . .

Victor objects to portrait painting for the same reasons as he objects to any painting to order, but I believe his reasons here are more subjective. Portrait painting doesn't suit him; he is sensitive to all that is fugitive and moody in a scene and hasn't much capacity for detached observation and constructing new order from hard facts, and the painted portrait doesn't interest him much, whoever has done it. . . .

At 10.15 Wendy, who had left us soon after we had taken our coffee, appeared quietly in the room. It was time to put the cats out and close the verandah door and say goodnight to friends, quietly so as not to disturb the children. The old late nights of our student gang days, reckless of sleep, do seem a long way off when one walks out of the calmly ordered and even decorous houses of the distinguished young painters.

1 May 1946

. . . Back to Rodrigo's for supper. While we were sitting in the kitchen at our meal Roland Pym walked in. The calmness with which we fell into a normal conversation on the eternal topics reminded me of the Paris school-man who after years of imprisonment returned to his students and began his first lecture 'As I was just saying'.

The war has been more of a gap to us than anything else and does not seem fundamentally to have changed any of my friends . . .

11 July 1946

. . . There is something very appropriate in the flaring brass chords in a cathedral – certainly in this one.[1] The assurance, the decision in colour and the firmness of tone, match the firmness of architectural shapes which don't wobble or fade out, which branch securely one from another and don't just make suggestions or gestures but occupy their space serenely, once and for all and with nothing vague about them, most exciting, even without the music and the occasion, to sit up there in a world of architecture, above, below, in front and behind and on both sides all you can see. Like being in a tree as a child; as exciting as that but much more satisfying. Most of the congregation up in the triforium seemed to be interested only in the King and Queen, there was no end of edging to the best vantage points, standing on benches and craning this way and that every time we stood up during the service. All the same they looked very nice and sensible people and seemed themselves to be intensely interested in the orchestra, the choirs and the trumpets, by no means solemnly gazing at their service books all the time.

. . . A cup of coffee with father and then up to London – not very comfortable journey, the train dreadfully crowded as far as Chatham but I was all the time in a wonderful mood of exaltation about the architecture of the cathedral and I see that I shall now be able to paint a few pictures that will be a great advance on any others I have done of it. I recalled those I painted and exhibited in 1933 when I must have been looking at it all as no more than a complicated and fretted decor, overlapping screens inside and outside, a tracery of contrasted rectangles and curves. There is a lot more I see now.

16 July 1946

No tobacco in the evening; rang up Victor and met him at the bottom of Eyot Gardens. He had a packet of Murrays mixture for me so we lit up and wandered off in the dark along Chiswick Mall and on through the gardens and recreation grounds as far as Barnes Bridge and back. We got to discussing commissioned work – what should be the contemporary artist's reaction and how he can deal with the problem. There are real problems even if one doesn't go very far in adherence to the priggish old idea of 'prostituting talent'. Victor put it all very clearly and with immense animation – talking on and taking no notice of where we went, whom or

[1] Canterbury Cathedral.

what we passed – delightful absorption and endless argument. For painters like ourselves, he argues, educated in the school of Cezanne, Post Impressionism and Cubism, where 'likeness' has not mattered beside other more important things, there is no tradition, not even a precedent, for painting a portrait or a landscape that can satisfy the client and remain still true painting to the artist. If the artist tries it he is right out on his own, must make his own way entirely from no known base, and must realise this position and go through with the task realising it all the time. This, Victor suggests, means that he can only take commissions from the very few people who share his own position, belong to his private world and will accept what it is he can give. The modern painter is essentially a private painter of course and V. would say that by becoming a professional portrait painter he of necessity becomes something different – his clients wanting a form of public art, popularly approved. If you find the right patron well and good – he takes what you like and he does not bother about a third spectator. How rare. V. is smartingly contemptuous of anyone who takes the line that today one can be a Goya or Rubens, tearing through a public, rapturous but partly blind, doing anything anyone wants and painting well at the same time. Only the general acceptance of a tradition of good painting by a large class of society, when mediocre painters have firm support and can do reasonable things and the great ones great things and still please, can make bespoke painting safe. Just take on a few such jobs, or do something else, to make a living; but take these jobs from the right quarter. Victor himself lives up to this very well so his opinion is worthy of respect. He has been commissioned to do two landscapes in Cambridge by the Dean of one of the colleges. His line is 'if you don't mind waiting a year, perhaps two, I shall look around in Cambridge, if I happen to have to go there for any reason, and if I like what you want me to paint well enough to make a couple of pictures there, I shall probably do something' – he would almost add 'taking jolly good care they will look nothing like the place itself'.

Victor Pasmore, 'View from Magdalene Bridge, Cambridge'

17 July 1946

St. George-in-the-East
National Monuments Record

On my way to Limehouse to see Hawksmoor's church there I met Bill who was at lunch in the National Gallery after another of his visits to the passport office. I went with him to Victoria where he had to make enquiries about his journey to France and in exchange he came on with me to Limehouse afterwards. Very well worth it, too. The church inside is unexpectedly magnificent – it is a fine space beautifully defined by its four columns, with a gallery round three sides and shallow chancel with a flattened arch, shallow but dark. The roof has all sorts of elaboration of plaster work in gold and white, rather coarse in detail, but magnificent in total effect, especially the huge central recessed circle. All the friezes are painted blue and this repeats beautifully in the roof the plan on the ground. And what a tower, a real passionate and yet subtly intellectual effort, splay-

St. George-in-the-East showing bomb damage. *National Monuments Record*

St. Anne, Limehouse. *National Monuments Record*

ing out at the bottom to give the effect of a continuing podium where the great parapet, walls of the stairways – north, west and south, reach out. Bill was very impressed too. He was off to paint his view in the city – after a cup of tea in an Aldgate tea shop he left me and I walked down to the Mint – good buildings about there, St. Katherine's Dock and the Mint itself – and along Cable Street looking for St. Georges-in-the-East. Not a very interesting walk until through a battered side street I saw the elegiac tower with its crown of truncated columns, wreathed with stone swags like trophies. Sad dilapidation round the base of the tower, everything is derelict. The church is gutted and a wooden hut for the services dumped down in it and other obstructions make it impossible to appreciate anything of the interior. Behind the church is a charming churchyard garden in a corner of which is an abandoned 'Nature Study Museum' – a small building through whose dusty windows I saw the empty aquarium tanks floored with dusty rockeries, a burst stuffed fish, a large green model of a frog with a tail. Beyond this is a trim and gay garden, well tended, a pleasant passage for people passing from Ratcliffe Highway to Cable St. From this end one can see why Hawksmoor made his towers wider N and S than east and west. From the east one can see them building up with the end of the church into a monumental vertical composition and being so wide the tower hasn't the effect of something fitted on to the roof. When you look at the side view of the church the contrast of vertical and horizontal is the main idea and it would be a mistake to have a wider tower – if it is high it might as well look high –

Well pleased with all this I looked at the Georgian houses in Cable Street and wandered on past huge tenement blocks and blitzed areas surrounded by high wire fences like abandoned concentration camps, down to Shadwell Basin – the church there is only interesting as a landmark from the river – and so back into Commercial Road and home.

18 July 1946

William Townsend, 'Sir Stephen King-Hall'

Tried my hand at an article on Paul Nash for the very simple but not stupid, possible-to-enliven public that King-Hall suggests might be appealed to.

After lunch I rushed out to Stepney again, starting from Aldgate and prowling about there for a little I made for Spitalfields, the third great monument of Stepney's Baroque golden age. There are some fine Georgian doorways in several of the streets round about and a superb shop front, truly noble and beautifully solemn in Artillery Lane. Christchurch was locked – it is cracking in places – the churchyard close in choked with shepherds purse and old decrepit men sit and lie asleep among the table tombs and family vaults. The east end is very good with its two flights of steps continuing the lines of the walls and the iron gates carrying these lines further still. As for the tower, as I walked back from it towards Bishopsgate I realised better how well and logically it builds up and made a

William Townsend, 'St. Alban, Wood Street', 1947

little drawing of it. The market men seemed surprised that anyone should take any notice of the church, and I was heartened by hearing one old chap say to another 'I love to see that sort of thing; first man I ever saw drawing round here; it's a lovely church'. That from a local makes up a little for the absurd neglect of these great churches by a great architect.

What neglect too and worse. I thought I would get off and look at St. Mary Woolnoth on the way back; included in the view of the lowest stage of the tower are a crowd of church notice boards, twelve underground posters, two huge metal signs with electric lighting provided for the underground, two more marked 'Entrance' (it is the entrance to the underground that is meant), and raised up on posts two more with 'Bank Station' as bold as brass.

I sauntered down to the desolate part of the city east of St. Pauls, lovely now with the church towers standing from the ruins of warehouses and wharf offices among the cellar pits overgrown with rosebay, ragwort and bracken. As I walked down Lower Thames St. I was hailed from an upper window. Bill was up there painting a view across the waste towards St. Mary le Bow. In five minutes time he came down, we admired the new scenery and had a drink and came home.

Letter from Anthony Bertram who for the last year has been employed by the British Council in Paris. During the war he was on air liaison with the Resistance movement and won all sorts of honours. He comes back to England next month and wants to give up lecturing and do creative writing.

13 August 1946

Summer exhibition at the Lefevre; more 'progressive' than show at the Leicester. I feel quite old to be wondering what the painters ten years younger than myself are getting at – it looks very much as though Cubism and Constructivism are being re-echoed in a curious debauched way in, paintings like these of Macbryde, Colquhoun and Minton; there are Picasso's and all sorts of other shapes figuring as no more than contemporary concessions in what is really not much more than a play of textures . . . These pictures, of which there are plenty more at the Redfern, seem to me entirely on the surface, even the romanticism doesn't go further because there is no other interest in things beyond their possibilities as shapes in which to work up a complicated effect of texture – that I find less interesting than using things as pegs for constructions – among this a large Sutherland and huge Francis Bacon look impressive, though both are nastily, unfeelingly painted. Basil Jonzen whom I met at the Redfern seems to be quite bewildered by what has happened since he was a much boosted and successful young painter . . .

27 October 1946

William Ratcliffe, 'The Artist's Room, Letchworth', *Tate Gallery*

Spencer Gore, 'The Cinder Path', *Tate Gallery*

28 October 1946

In the evening I called on William Ratcliffe, one of the few survivors of the Camden Town Group, who had a show recently at Delbanco's where I got his address. I saw a picture of his at the Letchworth show a year ago when I didn't know anything about him but recognized the work of an honourable painter. He lives in Wilbury Road in an untidy house, the home of an old friend, Stanley Parker who died this year and who was the father of three daughters – one of them Brynhild was at the Slade with me. He is a pleasant, tiny old man, with an egg-shaped head; looks like a wise old carpenter or cobbler shuffling about in a littered-up living room, then sitting by an open fire in a cottage armchair, and delighted to talk. He came to Letchworth 40 years ago, was encouraged to paint by Gilman who lived there too. Gilman built a house almost next door but never lived in it, but it was there that Spencer Gore lived one summer and did his pictures of Letchworth. Ratcliffe was one of the Camden Town Group from the start and remembers the gatherings at 19 Fitzroy Street and at Cumberland Market and the exhibitions at the Goupil. After the war (1914–18) he deplored the creation of the London Group when the 'cubists' swamped the old crowd completely. Then Gore was dead, and Gilman in 1919, and he confesses he has never painted so happily deprived of their stimulus and encouragement. He has gone on painting since, in the old tradition, but at his exhibition there was nothing painted much since 1925. The show was a failure though Raymond Mortimer wrote it up well, and the poor old chap is sad thinking of the huge bill for framing . . .

. . . At tea-time with Bill, Sam Carter and Monnington, M. gave us a remarkable, objective but nonetheless macabre account of the taking of Tonks's death mask, in which undertaking he was the assistant of Gerard. Monnington, who was Tonks's downstairs neighbour, the closest friend of his last days and in his illness, could not forget his friendly feelings even for the old man's dead body when the mask would not be detached from the face and he had to assist Gerard in a tug of war, first on the bed and afterwards as this did not allow for the exercise of all their strength, on the floor, for hours, to remove it. It was a very good mask apparently. Bill is most anxious to get a cast of it – he grows more and more attached to his days at the Slade, the doctrines of Tonks, his teaching and the memory of the master himself.

After supper to see Victor. He had just got back from Cambridge where he has made the first notes for a large landscape commission which after a good deal of fencing he had now decided to accept and carry out next summer.

2 February 1947

William Townsend, 'Isleworth'

Sir Thomas Monnington

18 March 1947

Long talk with Victor in the evening. Victor is a man who is not really interested in general ideas, general knowledge or wide casting speculation, unless these happen at some point to touch his immediate practice in painting. Then he is liable to involve himself in the tangles of some age old controversies, exciting himself about them as though they were new problems no one had thought of before. He is now concerned with definitions of reality because while he likes to consider himself a realist painter he is beginning to wonder whether he should properly be called so. Unlike Bill who is never happy when his eye is not fixed on the object he is painting. Victor starts this way but having reached a certain stage in his picture, when he has collected as much visual information as he feels he needs, he retires to his studio, carries on with his painting, making all sorts of alterations and additions to his version of the facts of nature – transcribing now a concept built up from his study. Or might it be simply a memory carried away, pure, of the object? Anyhow, now he would like to assure himself that a mental concept is as real, and in the same way, as physical actuality, so that he can paint from this concept and still be a realist.

The point I made as strongly as I could, and which is what matters, is that the painter's material, whether it derives directly from what he perceives or is based on an idea in his mind, must be something that can be truly expressed in shapes of various colours and tones. 'Sorrow' is not a suitable concept for painting – though it may be for music – 'sorrowing woman' could very well be – that would be a very much less profitable idea for a composer. Artists like Watts failed, I think, because they thought they could paint 'sorrow', 'hope', and so on.

Victor has started two new paintings of the river from Chiswick Mall – lovely beginnings where in the slightest indications of the main masses the accents of figures, beautifully drawn, are already spaced ready for the whole thing to be built up round them. Drawings for all the figures. Victor can't really conceive a figure in a way to paint it; he makes his drawing and though he cuts this about what he has seen and put down in the drawing is what counts all through, I think: and it is because he sees so much that his figures have a wonderful life and liveliness in their simple contours, not because he imagines and thinks liveliness into them as an afterwork.

Taught this evening – have exchanged my evening's work this week with John Dodgson so that I can be free on Friday. Tom Monnington was my colleague. We had a long walk beside the canal before tea; beautiful clear balmy spring air and light on the dingy pattern of industrial buildings, warehouses, wharves, pre-fabricated houses, tumbledown two storey streets. Monnington told me a lot about life on canal barges – he knows a great deal about that sort of thing; tough occupations, practical activities about which most of my own intimates are as ignorant as babes – or what they know is by intuition only. Monnington revels in the practical minutiae.

24 March 1947

Victor after our meal told us about a visit he and Claude made once to Sickert at Broadstairs.[1] To their surprise Sickert met them at the station; he even had a car for them. It was a five-mile trip and the car was very small. Victor got in first, Claude almost on top of him, Sickert's even greater mass on top of Claude, Sickert talked all the time. Victor couldn't hear a word but from his painful corner could see his head bumping up and down against the roof. At lunch Sickert said 'I've no idea who you boys are. You might be from the moon for all I know', but he was genial and communicative as long as his own work was under discussion.

Claude drank two or three glasses, Victor three or four and Sickert the remainder of five bottles of hock. Halfway through the meal Sickert started singing French songs and went on for a long time.

12 June 1947

. . . To-day was the private view of Claude's show at the Leicester Galleries which he shares with Edward Burra. Burra's pictures stared and clamoured from the walls but Burra himself did not appear; Claude with beard neatly trimmed and a huge rose on his chest gave an effortless display of an extrovert painter enjoying himself. His pictures look very well, unshakeably constructed and worked through to the end and no difficulties shirked. Nothing seems to deflect him from his concentration on the small ordered piece of world in front of him, he rarely seems to want either to alter or add to it, but he looks until he really sees a great deal about it. Of all the painters of talent to-day he must be the most convinced and happy realist. A good many pictures sold already – the Contemporary Art Soc. have bought the largest, a portrait of Marjorie Few sitting at a piano.

Met Michael Reynolds again after a gap of years. When I told him that I had listened to his war broadcasts from Italy and had always felt that he was enjoying the spectacle as he had enjoyed imaginary defences of Charlotte St. twenty years ago, he said this was quite true, he had enjoyed it so much that he was ashamed to be there at all.

6 October 1947

To the A.I.A. centre in the evening where the central committee members were assembled to greet the president of the Hamburg Artists' Union and his wife who are on a visit to the country as our guests. Frau Eirwan interpreted for her husband, who answered questions about the activities of the well-known German painters during the war and of the painters to-day. The Hamburg Union is not an exhibiting society but exists principally to maintain the legal and professional rights of 600 painters, pro-

[1] In 1934 Sickert had taken a house at St. Peter's-in-Thanet, near Broadstairs.

[74]

tecting studios from requisition and so on. It distributes an allocation of artists materials, all that is allowed by the Control Commission goes through it. The distribution has been two tubes of oil paint per artist in the last year; about two sheets of watercolour paper per month. The other sources are only pre-war stocks and black market supplies. The paint is manufactured in the British zone but most is exported to the Russian zone, where artists do much better for materials. The linseed oil comes from the Russian area in exchange. The Hamburg painters sell their pictures to people who have a balance of black currency they are afraid they may lose; so they buy pictures in order to have some realisable commodity. The currency reform will hit the artists badly. There is a desperate shortage, too, of reproductions and books of all kinds – we arranged to make a collection of small-scale prints of contemporary stuff for the Eirwans to take back. Teaching in the appreciation of art is impossible in schools where the children in any case have only microscopic pieces of ruled paper to draw on, if that. Mr Phillips, with whom the visitors are staying, said that both were very weak from undernourishment when they arrived; in fact, Eirwan himself has just come out of hospital after three weeks treatment for malnutrition . . .

17 October 1947

William Townsend, 'Street in Bayswater', 1948

Walk with Victor and Bill beside the canal at Peckham between afternoon and evening teaching sessions. We talked about the difference of attitude, especially of attitude to the objective world, between realist painters of our kind and the contemporary romantics or the idealists of the école de Paris. Bill, pointing to a crane, folded against one of the warehouses across the canal, stated like this the fundamental divergence between the painter interested first in a world outside himself and the painter interested in a world of his reactions with only the picture as an outside object. 'They start where we leave off. They believe they can draw that crane without any difficulty, the only problem is where to place it and in what picture. We are not sure we can draw it as we see it and the whole picture is our attempt to do so and we consider we have done well if we get somewhere near it'. We continued our discussion at tea in the Queens analysing the elements that are purely sense perception and those that are intellectual and imagined qualities added that make up what we accept as the reality of things outside. Studying the pepper pot and salt pot standing on the table we argued that the retinal image tells us only a small part of what we accept as the reality of these objects. They seem to have weight, and a solidity that is only understood by an intellectual interpretation of tone and colour changes on their facets; they have a space between them only apprehended because the shape of the shadow falling from one on to the other is seen not only as a tonal patch but as a shape defining the space, something one has learned and remembered, and so on. But all this is understood by direct contact with the objects themselves and of the space in which they are sited. This is the material of our paintings. The romantic painter at an early stage of his contemplation of such objects might feel that the two pots looked like two little people, two nuns perhaps walking in a snow covered field and at this stage would become more interested in this analogy and association than in the objects themselves, and try to capture only those aspects of the objects that would help him to express this feeling; or if an expressionist he would concentrate on certain qualities that would give the maximum expressiveness in some sense or another to the forms depicted. Bill says he tries to paint things 'not more nor less expressive than they are'.

15 December 1947

Victor came to Camberwell this morning to give the criticism of the life painting. He stood by the model's throne and delivered a carefully-prepared statement – half-reading it from notes – of the relation of the painted surface to reality; the theme being that it is not a question of copying lights and shades of imitation but of understanding and controlling the seen thing and then in lines, dots (I noted specially the dots, thinking of Victor's new pictures) making shapes on the canvas in which the object is re-identified. After this he was leaving the room amid applause without mentioning the canvases on the walls, which he had in any case said he would not criticise, without even awarding the prizes. But he came back and indicated two paintings for which prizes would be given and then we faced a number of people, as the students crowded in to dissect the exhibits, who were bewildered that the awards had not gone elsewhere – to pictures apparently so much more 'competent'. Skilful.

Victor's show[1] has been a great success. He has sold his pictures at high prices and has had considered reviews in all the papers and journals that matter; a rather carping one from Patrick Heron in the NS & N, but, clearly by someone so out of sympathy with any painting based on appearance that he could not really see the point, but others have noted that these are not only very beautiful and distinguished works, marking a stage in Victor's career, but have seen them as something much more important, as a research that has led to an enlargement of the pictorial vocabulary for commanding the objective world and its appearances; going on from Turner and Whistler and Seurat and getting at something new. What is really good about these latest pictures is that Victor has taken up and brought into circulation again some of those subjects and effects of very great beauty, of universally admitted beauty, that everyone responds to – the first star of twilight, mist over the water, moonrise and so on, that have been shunned by good painters for quite long enough.

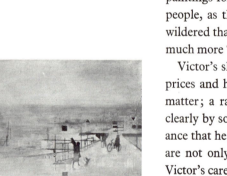

Victor Pasmore, 'The Evening Star', *Lord Clark*

[1] The exhibition was held at the Redfern Gallery, 27 November–27 December 1947.

12 March 1948

Long talks with Victor in the corridor outside the life room. He went to the Slade the other day to criticise the sketch club show there and said it was disgracefully bad and he treated it harshly. Lots of pretty sketches from nature and no one with even the intelligence to copy some other painter, he said. He gave the prizes to an imitation of a Bonnard and an imitation Matisse on the grounds that these students had at least looked at a picture. 'I don't believe in this looking at nature. Looking at nature never made anyone want to paint pictures. You only want to do it and learn how to by looking at other pictures'. These are pretty closely his words and this is an attitude he boasts of now. In fact he always does paint surrounded with reproductions and thinking of other pictures and yet even his earliest pictures show an extraordinary interest in particular things seen and a visual memory of appearances. He was already painting what he saw, even if he didn't look at the view all the time, when most painters would still be imitating the latest picture that had excited them. Bill always argues that Victor's best painting is done when he is trying to represent something that he has in front of him, and tries hard to save him from intoxication with aesthetic theories and the wiles of the self-styled or approved 'moderns'. In the same way Victor deplores the academic tendencies and caution in Bill that make him, out of respect for tradition, veer every now and again towards some group that seems to hold something of the tradition he admires however feebly and to be more honourable than the pretentious intellectuals who decree the fashion and make the current reputations. . . . What Victor admires is the bold and exact and natural architecture of Bill's early pictures and their lyrical feeling.

We had a great discussion of all this and of the uses and functions of art schools and academies and of the faults we commit in our own efforts at Camberwell. V. has little use for drawing in the life room and it is very rarely indeed that he gives an individual lesson there. He may walk in and glance round the drawings and say a word to an occasional student or he may in an authoritative way announce to the whole class some such remark as 'If the model has feet then draw the feet' and then walk out. He makes a more conscientious tour of the painting rooms but spends most of the time talking to Bill, Claude or myself in the corridors or discussing with some student in a corner, their work, the work of Seurat and the golden section and in this way he is a valuable instructor. Really no teacher he is a first class critic of other people's work. For students he is interested in, and that includes all sorts of freaks and duds, he is endlessly helpful and provocative. The rest he ignores entirely. As for me I give a dozen lessons perhaps in the liferoom; walk through the painting rooms and interfere as little as I can with Bill & Victor there unless I am asked for advice. Bill makes a conscientious round, gives a few drawing lessons and has always a few small jobs on hand, looking into the booking of models or the exam lists, that take him away and hide him in other parts of the school or in the secretary's or the principal's rooms. Probably the best teaching any of us do is usually the talking to some student in a corridor who brings a bundle of drawings or a sketch for a composition for us to see . . .

After the evening session went to Hammersmith to collect varnish and odds and ends and then by the last train to Letchworth with a small picture of Bill's under my arm.

14 April 1948

[On a visit to Victor Pasmore's new house at Blackheath] . . . Among the pictures Victor's four small 'abstracts'. The two most successful of these, which are unmistakable Pasmore's, have a Klee-like precision of organisation and are experiments with simple 'moving formats'. The better, an upright composition, is a spiral movement, on a green ground, of small triangles interspersed with rectangles, some of which are divided diagonally into two or four triangles, some distorted to emphasise the movement. The other is a horizontal movement, with clustered squares and triangles at one side thinning out to a tail on the right, like a game of Halma in progress. In the studio V. has a large work of a very different order; a scene in a park, based on sketches made in Greenwich and other parks; looking along a grey path which dips steeply into a dell in the bottom of which one sees the path spattered with figures proceeding through vivid lawns into a bank of trees of miraculous green. The trees are dealt with in the Rousseau manner, all the leaves and fronds worked out into an intricate pattern work. V. readily acknowledged the debt to Rousseau, and a few ideas from the French painter Le Franc who visited him and saw the painting a week or two back.

Only the other day I had remarked to Bill on my surprise that V. never showed the slightest interest in architecture and its aesthetics. Bill said 'He is bound to come round to it in time and some very strange ideas we shall get'. I told this to Victor when this evening he asked me to try to get a copy of the Architectural Review in which there is an article on the theory of modules and the golden section as employed by Le Corbusier . . .

1 May 1948

Met Bill at the National Gallery for lunch. I had promised to sit to him for a couple of hours in the Lord Chancellor's robes, so we went straight on to Westminster, penetrated into the Courts of the House of Lords and up to Jowett's suite. In the corridor the Chancellor himself, on the point of leaving for some appointment, bore down on us bending slightly from his truly majestic handsomeness, arm extended with aristocratic cordiality and invited Bill to make free of his office. A great room, in modern perpendicular, with three windows giving on to the Thames, decorated with a nice water-colour by Tonks, three larger and vapid ones by Dufy and others by Jowett's sister. Bill settled me in the robe, stiff black moiré surfaces encrusted with embroidery in wiry gold thread and there I sat for two hours while Bill screwed and stretched his eyes in agonies of penetration and balanced rulers on an extended finger in the search for statements of pure location, and in the course of it put down some fifty touches of yellow ochre and black to establish a fragment of the surface of one of the sweeping panels of the front of the robe.

11 June 1948

. . . In the afternoon Victor arrived, wearing a new white straw hat with a black ribbon. Had tea with him when he told me of a wrangle he had with Claude. Humphrey Brooke, since he saw the show at Letchworth, has had the idea of a Euston Road exhibition at the Tate and is prepared to push the idea. Claude is all for this; he longs to see the idea of the school, whatever it was, clarified, unmistakeably demonstrated as something quite different from academic naturalism, and indicated in an important show. Victor sees that this would tie everyone down to a line that never has been defined or agreed, that would have to be so vague that it could not be exclusive or of any value, or else artificially limited so that it would be a ban on progress. V. made it quite clear he would have nothing to do with such a show so there will not be one. In the meantime he has been invited to show in Paris at an exhibition of European abstract painting.

17 June 1948

There is an exhibition of work by Camberwell students hanging in the pub where we lunch. Over the counter hangs Gill's text 'The artist is not a special kind of man but every man is a special kind of artist'. This upsets Bill so much that he can hardly bear to drink while it remains – it is not the sentiment or statement he objects to, but the selfconsciousness of the demonstration. I defend it as a useful defensive opening in the attack on the locals. It is a text I used often in the army and found a valuable bridge to people only too aware of their separation from artists. Claude says 'why don't they say "A public house is not a special kind of house but every house is a special kind of pub".' . . .

3 July 1948

Took a picture to Brown for the Leicester galleries' summer show. In one of his rooms he has the new and fashionable strip lighting which made this picture look very hot and uncongenial. He doesn't think it is any good, but it is cheap and he says that the salesmen are so good that no one can resist them. Yet girls will walk round the side streets rather than be seen lit up like corpses in the glare from neon strips in public places; paintings are presumably less damageable than the complexion of the face . . .

3 July 1948

Hans [Hess] told me about Rohlfs' methods of work. This arose out of some discussion as to the artist's attitude to his subject and I had suggested, quoting Degas, that the artist painted best what he knew best, and had argued that what he had looked at often, whether in itself interesting or not, would be the thing bearing the greatest charge of experience and therefore most likely to be the subject that could produce the kind of picture that would survive repeated contemplation. I had been criticizing the kind of painting that has everything on the surface and nothing at a second view. Rohlfs he said, used to go to the seaside for the summer. His summer started in March and lasted for seven months. He would sit in a chair on a balcony looking at the sea all the morning, stop for lunch and go back to his chair for the afternoon. He would sit thus for three weeks or so and then in a couple of days produce a dozen water-colours of the scene. Then he would take a day or two off, visit another place and look around; after which he would come back to his balcony, move his chair to a new angle and sit again for the next three weeks. Hans considers him to be the only German artist of his time of major importance . . .

18 August 1948

Have just finished Geoffrey Grigson's book on Palmer. Though it is a panegyric of his earlier work, the whole account as well as the author's admission that the high poetic flights could not be maintained after P. was 30, seem to me to be a case against this kind of romanticism and to contain all the elements for criticism of the works themselves. The natural and spontaneous lyrical feeling of an excitable young man who grew up very slowly has been so deliberately over-stimulated it couldn't possibly last, – Grigson himself says the trouble was with Palmer that he could not develop his art, and of course not. It is a sort of hot-house, over-cultivated bloom, exotically lovely, short-lived and sterile. To me it is the dangerous kind of whipped-up sensibility leading to what Coleridge called 'pseudo-poesy'. It looks like genius if the artist dies at thirty, but when he goes on for another fifty years it looks like a fine talent sadly over-cultivated in a wasteful way. I should think Graham Sutherland must have realised this by the way he has been at such pains to free himself from the influences that were so overwhelming and clotting in his early etchings.

18 September 1948

Up early. In the Minster before breakfast, then the rest of the morning walking round York . . . York is much less messed about than any town in the south of England. As I walked along the canal with its brick factory buildings along the line of the walls and a whole industrial suburb to one side, it was as clear to me as any demonstration could be that industrialisation damages a fine place much less than twentieth-century commercialism. Various fine things disappear no doubt, but in their place buildings we put up that may be ugly in themselves, that make no pretence of being anything but utilitarian but that do not make any special attempt to attract attention to themselves – mills and factories and gas works are not exhibition stands or advertisements; and such as they are they fall into an urban landscape as structural features. Commercial development means that the buildings too join in a competitive struggle, each one has to assert itself, pull itself free from its neighbours, by colour, outrageous excrescences and decoration, advertisements of some kind or another; the shapes of good buildings are camouflaged, their surfaces defaced, structure everywhere is distorted and the whole scene reduced to a jittery texture in which nothing can be allowed to become a focal point. This happens to all high streets and outskirts of towns in the south. I suppose our new romantic illustrators – Michael Rothenstein, Minton and so on would see something to admire in these commercial scenic textures and have perhaps already caught something from this typical 20th century environment; perhaps it is only a matter of temperament that Bill, Victor and I would always be more moved by the more three-dimensional industrial landscape, however hideous. Maybe we really are children of the nineteenth century depaysés . . .

Near Walmsgate, just inside the city wall is an extraordinary surviving stretch of waste ground; very rough, pot-holed and hummocky, a string of old and dilapidated houses along one side – a thoroughly Borrovian site, with a number of small caravans, a few ponies, a tinker's low tent with bits of junk scattered round it; a ruined building used as some kind of work-shop. Distant view of the Minster and church towers.

Met Hans [Hess] at the gallery. Visitors to the exhibition about 150 per day. He took me home to lunch; a delicious meal cooked by Lily. Introduced to reblochon cheese which he told me used to be very fashionable on the continent in his youth and a favourite in his family. After lunch Hess and I walked for an hour or so along the river and he gave me his views on the English provinces. No hope he thinks of a real cultural centre anywhere in England outside London; all destroyed for good. Even Manchester could not support artists; can offer no background and nothing to feed on. Oxford & Cambridge might of course be exceptions. He mentioned a young sculptor who had called at the gallery this morning and shewn him photographs of work, very interesting, H. Said, after the style of Moore but rather further advanced, as far as H. was concerned quite as important and that may not be important at all; but he explained that in London with a Bond Street connection, in ten years he might become a world-wide name, written up everywhere; if he stays in York he will be an unknown teacher for the rest of his life and his work will gradually become less & less interesting. 'Of course it doesn't matter' H. remarked.

27 November 1948

Ben Nicholson, 'Still Life',
Tate Gallery

Lucian Freud, 'Girl with a White Dog',
Tate Gallery

Visited some of the galleries. At Delbanco's there are some very good Sickert drawings and small landscape panels, but they are not selling very well. Next door Victor's show is open, there were quite a lot of our students there in most earnest consideration, though the exhibition has its private view next Tuesday. There is the large park scene, a repainted early night scene from a window, three portraits, and most of the rest are 'abstracts'. I don't think they are good though they are beautifully disposed, the colour is lovely, the handling as good as it can be, but all Victor's good pictures have all these qualities and so much more; and I don't think the loss of the contact with real things and the density of objects and the lyrical feeling for them are compensated by the more explicit presentation of the structural thesis. Ben Nicholson, who has a show at the Lefevre, is giving up his non-representational line and paints views of St. Ives with lots of hills and boats dissected here and there. Some of his 'abstracts' made from assorted jugs and mugs on tables are beautifully done and gave me quite a lot of pleasure in other ways. The best picture I saw was a portrait by Lucian Freud at the London G. A small roomful of his work is almost lost in half a dozen shows – a houseful of absolutely worthless stuff. This portrait looks like the work of someone quite simpleminded – using simple in the right sense – pressed by the business of tracing out his subject in all its particularity, down to the last irregularity of the sitter's fingernails, and never flagging, convinced to the last moment of the importance of the job; and done with great skill. What is extraordinary is that with all this painstaking exactness and neatness the picture has a large rhythm, a sense of the whole thing in each part like an early Florentine portrait; – though German is perhaps a truer derivation.

5 January 1949

Painted, still life. Did some reading of Willis, on Canterbury Cathedral – a first rate biography of a building, of the stones themselves not what has happened inside the place. M. & I went to supper with the Daniels who have a pleasant flat in an early Victorian country villa at Blackheath. Claude and Elsie there too. Claude told a most amusing tale of Stanley Spencer, whom he met lately, giving a description of a large painting he is at work on now; so large he can only roll it in his room and unfold sections to complete at a time. It shows figures in attitudes of adoration, attitudes he said he had rarely seen or had an opportunity to study. He didn't feel like asking a model to adopt such unlikely poses as one would take up; so he tried to imagine the expressions and gestures he would like to find on people who really liked his pictures as much as he would like them to like them; then posed himself in front of a mirror throwing his arms and head about, exclaiming 'Oh Stanley what a wonderful picture' etc.

4 March 1949

With Victor . . . over tea – abstract painting, of course, and nostalgic reminiscence and examination of the objective abstraction phase. V. regrets that no one carried on from there, though if ever in all the history of painting there was a dead end there it was; abstract painting based on the play of pure sensibility carried to its logical end. There was no further step to take except Edgar's [Hubert] of reducing the colours used to black and white. V. now analyses with searching scrutiny every form of pure non-representational painting that has appeared, realises they are all lacking, and yet can be interested in nothing else – that is to say, interested in them as a pointer to his own next steps.

The Drawing Studio at the Slade School

The Antique Room at the Slade School

Teaching at the Slade
(July 1949–May 1951)

22 July 1949

Visited Bill at the Slade – the first time I have seen him installed there; though it is hardly installed to be landed in that shabby, disordered building, littered with ill-arranged files, dusty and uncatalogued pictures, rubbish and the most precious possessions of the place heaped together in odd rooms . . .

4 August 1949

Victor Pasmore, 'Abstract in White, Grey and Ochre', *Tate Gallery*

All the morning and until 3 doing a town plan of Canterbury for the book. Then to Blackheath to see Victor. He showed me three large collages he has just done, heavily framed and glazed but somewhat frail things in themselves. They are composed of pieces of newspaper – *Times* and *Daily Worker* – of cartridge paper, and odd pieces, very few, of coloured paper; mostly rectangular in shape, practically no curved shapes, pasted on white primed canvases. They have 'grown', slowly but with few revisions, Victor says; one of them had, however, been planned and the design done in charcoal on the canvas and then filled in with paper. The colour and tone range is very subtle and narrow – white, off-white, cream. I can't think what will happen as the paper discolours but Victor says he has allowed for that. He is very modest about them – says he is doing collage only as a step towards painting; at this stage he does not feel happy about painting such large surfaces of non-representational shapes, he brought out a fourth, rather shyly 'This one is no good. It was rather ambitious and I can't manage that yet'. It had pieces of foil paper in its make-up that took the light, reflected it and altered the pattern like the gold backgrounds of Byzantine work.

Wendy was out with the children. Victor made tea and we sat in the long room that stretches from the front garden to the back, full of light, rush mats, low furniture – a Japanese touch – and discussed Chinese and medieval aesthetics. Medieval art is Victor's latest discovery . . .

Walking back to the station across Blackheath we examined the problems of realism in turn. The trouble, according to Victor, is that we have no way of painting the wooden quality of wood or the leafiness of trees; we are not people who can start from scratch; all brought up as abstract painters – à la Matisse – we are bound to go on from there; we can't get to realism from Matisse or we get a mere padding out of formulas . . .

Victor Pasmore, 'Square Motif, Blue and Gold: The Eclipse', *Tate Gallery*

10 August 1949

David Jones, *David Jones Trustees*

David Jones, 'Mass', *David Jones Trustees*

. . . This afternoon Bill took me to meet David Jones who lives in Harrow-on-the-Hill where he has a large room in a kind of boarding house kept by a former master of Harrow School. Here he lives a sedentary and rather secluded sort of life with some degree of friendly oversight in the intervals between his frequent breakdowns. A mild-mannered, rather puddingy little man, with soft, pasty, irregular, face; not a healthy-looking man, but he doesn't seem an unhappy one; a little uncertain, but I should say only the uncertainty of a naturally shy, introspective man who has learned to get on with people. He was very friendly to us, entirely without pretence or formality – one could imagine how gay and amusing he might be with close friends. From the window of his room he looks deeply down into a garden with a few large trees reaching from a foreground tangle of fences, outbuildings, the school rifle range and smaller trees; opening to views of pastures and clumped oaks with London in the distance – the view that inspired most of the drawings in his last show and a number of others that he had in his room. Enmeshed in their rather spidery web of all-over decorative drawing – decorative in effect to me, though I doubt if any line is pure decoration to him; more likely full of some mystic purpose – are patches of most beautiful and distinguished straight drawing. 'Once you've learned to draw you can just draw anything. I am worried about how things ought to be drawn; I don't know whether they ought to have a black line round them or what – to draw how I feel about them' . . . He showed us an extraordinary drawing of the performance of Mass; – how he feels about Mass; the space and arrangement of the church, of objects and of persons conducting the service are those he sees from his usual position in church – he hastened to remember this part of the composition, but every object is freely transformed into something quite new; swirling, smoking, curling into every possibility of evocative and symbolic detail. When we arrived he was writing – on his bed. On boards were laid out several sheaves of manuscript, a map, a few books in formal neatness. On his walls he has the O.S. maps of Roman and Dark Age England, a geological map of England – these may belong to the house but he seemed very interested in them – and a plan of Caewent. We had a schoolroom tea, at an immense oval table, spread for many more than the three of us and the host, with a huge pyramid of small rock buns in the middle.

6 October 1949

Michael Rothenstein went into the London Gallery the other day. The advanced young man who is always reading books on obscure contemporary artists, told him that their next show would be of works by Matta; then lowering his voice to an almost confidential whisper added, 'You know Matta ? Matta of the New Reality'.

15 December 1949

The Slade dance in the evening. Fancy dress was obligatory. Last night Eric de Maré and his wife and I created an imaginary character for me to act, building him around a little fur cap Vanessa had and a blue towel bathrobe left in her cupboard by a visitor. I was an ex-Oxford Persian, maintaining shabbily something of the Oxford tradition after twenty years as a teacher of English in a Near Eastern provincial town! Bill's costume was less subtle and required less ambitious efforts at acting – evening dress with a huge ginger beard.

Colquhoun and Macbryde gate crashed on the dance at about one in the morning. The students let them in and they floundered and argued about the school for some time. Then they appeared in Bill's room where several of us were gathered about the drinks on the table. Both were fairly well dazed, but glad to have more drinks and fairly amiable until, as the party woke up, Macbryde shouted 'Come along out of this, Robert, don't let the bloody English get hold of you. Come along out I say', and they bundled off...

In the afternoon I went to Charlotte's school concert and party. Charlotte did a recitation, sang in a carol choir and performed in a figure dance with plenty of self possession and not much need for prompting.

7 February 1950

William Coldstream

Slade School of Fine Art

Tom Monnington took Bill and me to the RA this afternoon where we were to select, from among the paintings and drawings left by Walter Russell in his studio at his death, one or two things that could hang as a memento at the Slade. We were taken, from the deepest basement, up a short flight of stairs to a gloomy vaulted cavern, divided into two, all along one side of the larger room and all the way round the smaller one were stacked scores of canvases from smallish landscapes to large portraits; clumps of framed watercolours and echelons of 'important' pictures in heavy gilt frames; piles of drawings on a table, hundreds of small panels on the floor – all alike collecting the dust. It was not so much the contemplation of this huge amount of unwanted work as the dimness of the works themselves that was disappointing. It was difficult for any of us – even for Tom – to find much to admire in the portraits. They had the air of the period of Steer, McEvoy and Tonks and nothing at all more lasting; the landscapes all the themes of Steer in a watered echo, and that is watery indeed; – every phase of Steer too, from the Dieppe beaches to the pseudo Constables, Severn Valleys and so on; the sea shore at Walberswick, the watercolours of sails lost in sea haze. We chose a self-portrait – very close in arrangement to Tonks's self-portrait with legs folded under the chair – which had besides its interest as a portrait, some respectable painting in the head and a feeling, behind, of the gentlemanly untidiness of an academician's painting room and the yellow light of a London Edwardian interior; then a watercolour and a few of the small oil sketches which have more than survives in any of the painting. We also salvaged Max Beerbohm's drawing of Steer. Tom was very depressed by the whole excursion and I tried to comfort him by suggesting that it was no great matter if three-quarters of a painter's work accumulated as waste to be abandoned at his death – perhaps it would be better to destroy something from time to time – if one painting in four was really worth keeping. But he was really miserable. This was just the wrong stage of his career for him to see and have to acknowledge the collapse of an eminent academician's reputation as justified.

1 March 1950

Fernand Léger, 'Leaves and Shell', *Tate Gallery* © S.P.A.D.E.M. Paris, 1976

With M. to the Tate to see the Léger show; complete survey from before the Cubist period to this year; the more or less Cubist pictures are attractive but not very clearly thought-out Cubism; about the rest there is nothing very attractive, in fact many of them I find hideous and some of the latest of all pointless to the extent of being little more than barbarous decorations; but I feel a kind of compulsion about the paintings of the '20s, the machine turned women, the window bars out of Mondrian and the mechanised landscapes behind. They work, and with such vigorous simplicity and directness of statement and with such incredible assurance; if they are not satisfying sensuously they are at least like a hefty purge for the eye and mind; left the show feeling I did not want to see any fluffy by-products of impressionism and out of humour with my own painstaking progress of trial and error, or the beautiful hesitations of my friends (which of course are not the fluff that is so tiresome) . . .

18 April 1950

Lucian Freud, 'Self-portrait', *Tate Gallery*

. . . This evening Bill took me along to Lucian Freud's home in St. John's Wood to have drinks in celebration of his show, which opens to-day . . . Eduardo Paolozzi . . . shewed us into the front room, where the two high windows were heavily curtained to keep out the daylight. All the furniture was cleared except one large red-plush-carved settee, two screens, one of them carved in tiger skin, and a table from which were served champagne and whisky. This was a company in which Bill and I were like strangers, matter of fact and banal. There was Lucian's exquisite silent little wife and only one other woman, the wife of a huge bearded man. The rest of the men were beautifully hairless, smoothest of all a young man so preciously and delicately turned out, a pupil of Cedric Morris's, whom it would be impossible to caricature. Had a long talk with Francis Bacon who is fantastic enough, but charming and immensely intelligent.

22 April 1950

Have done some drawings the last few days and made a little beginning again. There is a subject come across in walks and cycle rides round here that I want to make drawings of – the newly-strung hop alleys. There are

[88]

many variations in the stringing, giving different sections to the alleys and different series of shapes cutting the sky between the poles. The systems built on permanent rows of poles have not in this district superseded those built on removable poles, as they have round Canterbury. Here there are string alleys between the thick permanent poles, single ones and double – the most fascinating of all – where the poles are very wide spaced; there are alleys strung from movable poles placed vertically as well as others between poles planted in pairs leaning outward in acute angled Vs . . .

16 May 1950

Professor A. H. Gerrard

London . . . McWilliam told me an amusing anecdote about Gerrard. Stories about him are innumerable, entertaining and usually true, for he is a natural eccentric, as fantastic but more amiable than Beckford. About twenty years ago he came to a decision as to the style of dress he should wear, sports jacket, corduroy trousers, yellow waistcoat, yellow stock. He went out and bought a dozen pairs of corduroy trousers, half a dozen yellow waistcoats and a supply of yellow stocks. He has varied his sports jackets from time to time but otherwise has subsisted on this wardrobe until to-day, satisfied with his plan. He has now worn out the trousers and has bought a pair of grey flannels.

17 May 1950

William Townsend, 'Hop Alley'

Went with Claude this afternoon to see the work submitted for the Prix de Rome . . . There couldn't be any doubt that the two Tonys are in a class on their own. There is not much sign of anything but art student competence in the rest, and little enough of that. A student from Bristol, Folkes whom I gave a prize last year, has something – at least he had been well taught; but his composition is a misguided return to the Nazarenes. Tony E's. [Eyton] picture disappointed me in detail – the principal figures were clumsy and not very distinguished in any way, but the planning of the thing was highly intelligent and had a sort of calculated nobility. Tony Fry's is admirable indeed. He seems to be the only painter there who was touched by the theme of the betrayal and nothing of the grave poetry he felt has been lost. It is too a completed work – that was made possible perhaps by his doing it almost in monochrome – with very beautiful passages of mountain background, of mid-distance figure groups that are only part of a consistently beautiful thing. The British School at Rome might become something worth while with these two there.

Met Michael Salaman at the show. Robin Darwin nearly ran over us all three just outside as we strolled off talking into the road.

26 October 1950

. . . Spent the afternoon revising my script, then went to see Victor. John Dodgson was there – just about to leave after a tea-time visit. They were arguing about Victor's generalisation that the great break, in modern paint-ing, from the tradition can be summarised as the end of interest in light and shade. Interest in light and shade began, says Victor, only after Giotto and lasted to the Impressionists, – infecting Cubism a little; now dead; as dead as in Japanese prints or Egyptian art. Victor stated all this as a fact. John was very worried – he thinks of light as the essence of good painting. He saw there might be a difference between light and 'light and shade', but was still worried. Victor now has, hanging and standing by the bookshelves in the long room, enough new 'abstracts' to make a show; the shapes are no longer limited to rectangles and triangles but, as he said, he has tried to invent more complex shapes 'and it isn't easy'. There are several very beautiful ones composed with spirals. Also saw the drawings and a model showing the design *in situ* for the tiled decoration V. is doing for a restaur-ant in the 1951 exhibition; a vastly enlarged drawing, in black white and grey lines of a waterfall. The design is derived from drawings (of the sea) done by Victor during the summer at St. Ives. A good many of the draw-ings he did there have been turned into lithographs too, extremely simple designs of houses, rocks, cliffs and spiralling shapes of water, re-drawn on transfer paper from sketches made on the spot. The most completely Victorian exhibits, however, were the two nudes painted long ago and now being embellished or 'completed'. That belonging to Lady Clark has had Victor's own head in the corner changed into the likeness of Ingres and the inscription 'The Studio of Ingres' painted in above it. This happy idea has led V. to turn the other (the Contemporary Arts Soc's nude), now almost entirely repainted and indeed re-composed in almost every detail, into 'Titian painting'. Titian himself does not yet appear but I gather he will do so. Victor is now able to dismiss these two paintings as academic exercises and seems to be satisfied that the post-dated inscriptions will prove that this is what they have always been.

Victor Pasmore, 'The Snowstorm: Spiral Motif in Black and White', 1950–51, *The Arts Council of Great Britain*

Victor Pasmore, 'The Studio of Ingres', *Lord Clark*

27 October 1950

Wyndham Lewis

To the Slade to meet Bernard Denvir whom I had invited to lunch. Took him to the British Council place in Davies St. where Mrs Somerville had asked me to meet Wyndham Lewis and a young negro painter in whom Lewis and the British Council were both interested. We all lunched to-gether, with Eric Westbrook and Hulton – at British Council's expense. Williams, the painter in question, comes from British Guiana; he was at Camberwell for a year, though he didn't paint there, a couple of years ago and we just remembered each other. Finding no chances of teaching in Guiana or of earning a living otherwise than as a clerk, he has brought a batch of pictures to London and is trying to launch himself here. We saw some of his pictures afterwards in Portland Place; they are immensely talented; powerful, crude, only half-formed perhaps, the latest ones a good deal influenced by Mexican socialist realism and by the work of Wilfredo

Lam. Lewis is large, white-faced, and much milder in speech and manner than his writings would suggest. He has small features, small mouth, nose distinctly too small and questioning, intelligent, very dark small eyes. Whenever I spoke they fixed me, not unkindly but with sharp, exploring attention and it seemed important not to talk nonsense. His talk was entirely unshowy, bang on the nail all the time, clear and full of sense. His published criticism so often seems full of bitterness, and even irresponsible, but to-day he was the responsible elder statesman of the party and almost benign in a dry, unillusioned sort of way . . .

3 November 1950

William Townsend, 'Hop Alleys'

Started a 30 × 25 canvas from another of my hop-garden drawings. At least I think all the preparatory scratching around and moaning over the drawings has had some effect. Anyhow now I think I see how to paint the thing. Colour entirely from memory or invented; no good trying to paint these alleys as I see them and want to explain them from the 'effect' – indeed it is a subject that could hardly be tackled from an impressionist point of view even by painting on the spot. Though everything is there when one sits and looks into the alleys as I have done to draw them, it is not by simple *coup d'oeil* that the pattern of the strings and the understanding of the deep structures made entirely of lines come together to make their extraordinary impression. Effects of light are really of no importance at all; not only light and shade contrasts don't matter, but the sense of light in the whole scene is not much to the point.

13 November 1950

. . . Back at Cartwright Gardens I stepped into a roomful of students in a high state of excitement concocting plans for waylaying Picasso at the private view of his show tomorrow and persuading him to come along to the Slade.[1] I calmed them down a little and suggested they should be patient until the morning and ask Bill to ring Penrose and find out what Picasso's movements might be.

14 November 1950

Cartwright Gardens, London WC1

We found out who was making the master's plans for him and when Picasso's train was due from Sheffield. Two of the students, Barbara Braithwaite and Heckford, went off to meet him at St. Pancras. They seem to have done very well. Just as Picasso was alighting from the train Barbara was handed by an unknown lady a bunch of red carnations. 'You give them to him' and she did – as from the 'étudiants de l'école des beaux arts Slade'. The result was that they were allowed to accompany Picasso to his taxi while Rodrigo and a large body of Royal College students couldn't get a look in.

[1] *Picasso in Provence*, Arts Council exhibition at the New Burlington Galleries.

[91]

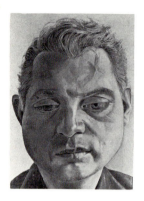

Lucian Freud, 'Francis Bacon',
Tate Gallery

Francis Bacon came to lunch. Bill took us to the Casa Prada where the customers entering through the swing doors then pushing curtains aside and coming into the restaurant behind a glass panelled screen were a perfect tribute to the guest. Francis gave us some wonderful illustrations of the things that interest him, 'a trap set out and a smear across it, a kind of slime, showing that a human being had passed through'. This may not be the best of how he feels; he is a very intelligent and comprehending man as well as one with extraordinary and perverse intuitions.

We went down to the Picasso show at the New Burlington Galleries. Bill and I each had cards for two so we took Francis and Michael Heckford. All the Arts Council and British Council people, the press and plenty of artists were there with half an eye for a perfunctory survey of the work and most of their eagerness for the expected appearance of Picasso, but he didn't come. I spoke to Gabriel's [White] wife who told me he had made a statement that he would have nothing to do with the Arts Council as it was a body dependent on the government that had wrecked the Sheffield conference and that he had cancelled his part in the plans it had made for him. Sad for Gabriel who has worked hard to make just the arrangements that would suit him, with a drinks party of just the people summoned from everywhere that Picasso has asked to meet. Someone might have explained that the Arts Council and MI5 are not really very closely connected, but perhaps this is the only form of protest he could make.

20 November 1950

... Sylvester – art critic and formerly secretary of Henry Moore – came to see us and look round the school. He is regarded with some awe in certain quarters and with a good deal of irritation in others – much as Douglas Cooper might be. However, we took him to see the students' sketch club exhibition that was hanging up and I should say he was the most perceptive and catholic visitor we have introduced. Not many people who aren't painters see the point of paintings so immediately and surely as this. He went up a lot in our regard. Bill remarked that he talks and thinks of nothing but painting. So he will have to be treasured ...

29 November 1950

Piper and Moore were both at the Slade to-day as visitors; Robert Melville came in to lunch and at the last moment we found we knew of no place where we could sit agreeably so many at a table and talk. Gerrard with a splendid gesture invited us all to the French Club in Cavendish Square. We got into a couple of cars; Jerry treated us to sherry while the table was prepared and then to a couple of bottles of Beaune with an admirable lunch. The time went on and Bill had to telephone back to the Slade to put off first one student, then another who had appointments to see Piper, while we went on talking – mostly about sculpture, the new Italians Manzù and

Marini, and Moore described his impressions of shows in Paris of Arp and others. He had nothing to say for the painting being done there now and said he left the Musée de l'Art Moderne disappointed, depressed and indeed disgusted with the whole business of painting.

Moore's comments are admirable, they are direct, clear and sensible and without pretensions of certainty where he isn't sure. He has the penetrating commonsense that Sickert had, as well as the intuition for a revealing phrase of summary that lets you know a creative mind is at work . . .

9 January 1951

Stanley Spencer, 'Double Nude Portrait: the artist and his second wife', *Tate Gallery*

Tom told me to-day the story of Munnings' campaign against Spencer. Apparently it arose from animosity towards Kelly in the first place and was quite deliberately calculated to embarrass Kelly after he had invited Spencer back to the R.A. Munnings knew of the questionable pictures, most of which were held by Tooths and had been for years shown only to trustworthy amateurs, though one was hanging in a club and thus could be considered to be on public exhibition. Munnings went to Tooths and inveigled from them photographs on the incredible grounds that he thought the Chantrey might be interested in buying them. He is said to have shown the photos to both Archbishops who, gentlemen at least, turned away. He then produced them at Newmarket to the Commissioner of Police and asked what he was going to do about them. Appealed to by an ex-president of the RA doubtless he felt he must take some action. Anyhow the owners in a panic, though presumably unnecessary, destroyed the works. The whole affair was put about in the press just to make a bad smell . . .

22 January 1951

. . . I notice that far more sophisticated and self-conscious students also are far less enthusiastic than we were about the work of near contemporaries. They avoid better on the whole the craze to be 'modern' but they seem to be incapable of the plunging enthusiasms that were exciting and useful to us. A few students are keen investigators of Klee or Picasso, but these are almost old masters to them. I never get news from a student of any younger painter he has discovered for himself.

15 March 1951

Sat at Bill's table with Frank Ormrod's daughter one side and Victor Willing's wife on the other, with Stanley Spencer opposite [Slade dinner]. I came, at the end of too long a toast list, to respond for the staff, most ambiguously honoured and at great length by Willing. I proposed Stanley Spencer which proved a popular inspiration. He got up and rambled on charmingly and quite amusingly but to one or two tables only – very few could hear him. He paid a tribute to George Charlton, and told us how when he (Spencer) first came to the Slade at the age of 19 his father came five or six times with him to see him safely across the Euston Road and make sure he could manage the crossing. He had had traffic drill from his earliest days but only in Cookham where there was practically no traffic.

[Martin] Froy proposed [Prof. Rudolph] Wittkower, made a very good speech and pleased W. very much by describing him as an 'august personage'. There was a crowded coffee party at Cartwright gardens afterwards with a close knot of admirers round Stanley Spencer. We persuaded Jerry to take some of us down to Camberwell where Dick Lee was celebrating. He has got the Abbey Major award this year, with Francis Hoyland as one of the Abbey Minor prizewinners. We found his basement in Wilton Road – Tony Fry's house, – a real nursery for the School at Rome. There were quite a lot of Camberwell students we had known all grown a little larger and older; Pat George, Andrew Forge, Rodrigo and Elinor as distinguished guests and Bill and I were made very welcome. There was plenty of energetic jiving and jumping about, a wonderful sense of physical liveliness and good spirits and somehow much more feeling that it was good to be young and an artist than we find at the Slade. At the Slade the students seem more consciously gentlemen or more conscientiously students than here, though they can on occasions be jolly enough. I can see them thinking of themselves as art teachers managing their lives sensibly and painting steadily; there is too much business of getting qualifications, or too portentous a realisation of the importance of academic studies, general knowledge, man-of-the-worldliness, and though there are no doubt as many good and serious artists among them there doesn't seem any of the feeling of excitement about the business of painting and general fun of life that I at once notice at Camberwell. Perhaps it is that Camberwell is like a tight little island where everything is concentrated, inwards to a small group who set the tone. Anyhow there is a good, healthy, serious, enjoyable sort of kitchen air about a crowd of Camberwell students . . .

18 April 1951

Claude Rogers and William Townsend

Claude took me in the lunch hour to the New Burlington galleries to see the sixty pictures painted at the invitation of the Arts Council. They hang there for the press to see before their first showing in Manchester. The first impression is that the idea has been fully justified by the fact that at least a third of the artists have produced very good examples of their work that might otherwise never have been painted. Claude's picture is surprisingly successful. Far from looking the laborious and worthy essay of a dowdy painter that it might have seemed it holds the wall in its sophisticated company with great confidence; the design seems quite majestic if academic, the colour quite noble . . . the downfall of most of our respected elders is sadly apparent – Matthew Smith and Ben Nicholson are the exceptions. We learned that the announcement of the five pictures to be bought by the Arts Council for £500 apiece would be made in the gallery at four

Claude Rogers, 'Miss Lynn',
Southampton Art Gallery

o'clock and arranged with the girl to ring through to the Slade then. So back at the Slade Claude began to prowl round the office near the telephone at about a quarter to four, not perhaps expecting a prize but thinking his own picture was in the running. The call came through and the phone was handed to him and I stood by while he poised his pencil to note the results on a pad of paper already numbered from 1 to 5. 'What! No! Really!' and other ejaculations and then he wrote against figure 1 'Rogers'. He could barely keep patience to follow up with the names of Hitchens, Freud, Medley and Gear. We gave him a clap and off he chased across the college to cash a cheque. He was soon back with three bottles of champagne which those of us lucky enough to be in the office happily drunk to his success. He has already decided to spend part of his five hundred in a first visit to Italy . . .

Index of Names

The numbers given after the names indicate the pages on which references to them appear. The pages on which there are illustrations are shown in italics.

Where it is particularly relevant to the material in the Journals brief biographical details have been given, wherever possible.